A PALISADES CONTEMPORARY ROMANCE

SPIRITS

Peggy Darty

PALISADES

SPIRITS
published by Palisades
a division of Multnomah Publishers, Inc.

© 1998 by Peggy Darty
International Standard Book Number: 1-57673-460-9

Cover illustration by C. Michael Dudash
Design by Brenda McGee

Scripture quotations are from:
The Holy Bible, New International Version (NIV) © 1973, 1984 by International Bible Society, used by permission of Zondervan Publishing House

Palisades is a trademark of Multnomah Publishers, Inc., and is registered in the U.S. Patent and Trademark Office.

Printed in the United States of America

For information:
MULTNOMAH PUBLISHERS, INC.•POST OFFICE BOX 1720•SISTERS, OREGON 97759

Library of Congress Cataloging-in-Publication Data:
Darty, Peggy.
   Spirits/by Peggy Darty.
      p.cm
   ISBN 1-57673-460-9 (alk. paper)
   I. TITLE.
PS3554.A79S65   1998   98-29214
813'.54–dc21   CIP

98 99 00 01 02 03 04 — 10 9 8 7 6 5 4 3 2 1

He will command his angels concerning you to guard you in all your ways.

PSALM 91:11

M ichael was thinking of Elizabeth, longing to be with her instead of trudging through the back trails of the Smoky Mountains. He stared down at his worn hiking boots, wondering how long he and Ben Thornton, his guide, had been walking. He began to suspect they were hopelessly lost.

Suddenly Ben nudged him. "Look!"

Michael lifted his head and squinted through the sunlight. Just ahead, a quaint log cabin nestled on the edge of the woods. The cabin appeared to be occupied. An old rocking chair sat on the porch, and calico curtains framed the windows. Slowly the door opened, and both men stopped walking as a young woman stepped out. She was dressed in tan doeskin with matching moccasins, and her dark hair was plaited neatly in braids on each side of her face.

Michael rubbed his weary eyes and blinked. "Is she real, or did we just fall back into the last century?"

Ben's voice was low and gentle, the tone he used when trying not to frighten a creature of the woods. "Either she's real, or she's our guardian angel. Either way, she's the most beautiful woman I've ever seen."

ONE

I can't believe we're in Angel Valley," Elizabeth said to her husband, Michael. She was fidgeting on the front seat of their car, looking every bit as delighted as their little daughter, Katie, on Christmas morning. It always amused Michael that while being one of the most intelligent women he had ever known, Elizabeth often displayed a little-girl amazement when caught up in a new situation.

"Well, we *are* here," he confirmed and felt a sense of excitement as well. He looked from right to left at the neat little town that had managed to retain the aura of a small mountain village despite the subtle update of its architecture. Where there had once been frame and concrete, carefully designed cedar-and-shake exteriors dressed up the hardware store, post office, drug store, and groceries. One of the old service stations had been replaced with a newer one, but the other one still held the imprint of years gone by.

Straight ahead, layered against the horizon, were the Smoky Mountains. An early morning mist shrouded the tips of the mountains in a pale blue haze, adding to their mystique.

"It's good to be here," Michael sighed. "Should we really mix business with pleasure? Maybe we should just forget we've come here to help find a missing woman. Wouldn't it be a lot more fun just to be happy, carefree tourists?"

"Oh, sure it would." Elizabeth gave him a wry glance. "But you don't for a moment expect me to believe you would fail to take your job seriously, Michael. Besides, we can do both." She snuggled closer to him. "We can be happy tourists, and we can find Mary Chamblis as well. I have faith."

"I love you," Michael said, glancing from the road to the woman who was so dear to him.

She was wearing a royal blue warm-up suit with a white turtleneck, and Michael appreciated her beauty. Looking at her, you'd never guess she'd been the victim of a hit-and-run accident a few months ago. His heart ached as he recalled the danger that had surrounded her for a while, but now Phillips was behind prison bars, and their life had returned to normal. Elizabeth had gained her weight back, and with her wheat blond hair dipping about her shoulders, Michael thought she had never looked more appealing.

He reached across and squeezed her hand. "You know I'm a sucker for a case, particularly one as intriguing as this."

Elizabeth frowned. "Sorry, hon, but I don't see what's so intriguing. A man and woman go on a hike in the mountains; she walks down a trail to look at the view and never comes back. Sounds to me as though she fell off one of these mountain peaks and the search-and-rescue unit just overlooked a hidden cove. These valleys are so deep; I can see how that would happen. These are the oldest mountains in America according to the tourist brochure."

Michael shook his head slowly. He always had a sixth sense about cases, particularly the details that seemed to be overlooked by others. "Fortunately I met Matt Wentworth in Atlanta at a fund-raiser two years ago," Michael said, surveying the pretty little town. "When I telephoned two days ago, he remembered me. Since he and his wife own a shop here, he's in a position to hear a lot of the local buzz. Matt says there's something really odd about this case, but he can't put his finger on it. That's the kind of statement that intrigues me."

Elizabeth reached over to affectionately smooth back a lock of dark brown hair from Michael's forehead. When he turned to face her, his blue gray eyes glinted with amusement.

"And you want to be the one to find the missing piece to the puzzle."

She was smiling as her eyes traced the familiar profile of her husband's face. They had been through so much together—a separation, a hit-and-run that left her with amnesia until Michael captured the criminal and her memory returned. Since then, however, their lives were back to normal, and they were now closer than ever. With a tiny sigh of appreciation, she looked at the lean face with wide, blue gray eyes, slim nose, and full lips. His hair was thick and soft, and she knew exactly how it felt on her fingertips. He was dressed in comfortable jeans and a white cable-knit sweater. *Thank you, God, for blessing me with our reunion...and for Katie as well.*

"Look at those guys." Michael inclined his head toward her side of the window.

A strand of hair tickled her cheek as Elizabeth swung around and looked out the window. She lifted her hand, absently pushing her hair into place as she concentrated on the view. They were passing the town square, where older men sat on benches, talking, dreaming of younger days, petting a dog that looked as old as the men.

"It's as though we've dropped back to the forties," Elizabeth said, shaking her head in amazement.

"How do you know what the forties were about?" Michael teased. "You weren't even a thought then."

Elizabeth swatted playfully at his right shoulder. "Grandmother kept a very good scrapbook. And I've seen movies set in the forties."

He nodded. "Okay, so you know about the forties. As for

the look and feel of the place—" he paused, giving the little town another once over—"you're right, you know. It does seem as though we've dropped back in time in one sense; on the other hand, there's enough improvement to the buildings to preserve them. And, of course, there are a few nice additions, such as this one."

Michael was turning into a parking space before an impressive corner building. It was a sprawling structure of cedar, with lots of glass through which one could see counters of various arts and crafts displayed.

"This is Matt and Laurel's place," Michael announced. "I told him we'd stop in when we got to town, but I wasn't sure exactly what day that would be."

Elizabeth was only half listening as her eyes scanned the interesting displays of baskets, wall mats, and colorful afghans. "I can't wait to wander around inside."

Michael cut the engine and removed the car keys. "Pretty neat place, isn't it?"

"It certainly is." Elizabeth grabbed her purse and hopped out, tilting her head back to study the shop. The exterior looked and smelled new, and she had already heard from Michael the staggering amount of money that Matt had invested in it. She also knew that Matt was wealthy and could afford to construct whatever kind of building he chose. The amazing thing was that he had chosen to invest in a quaint little town in order to preserve the variety of mountain talent.

"Look at this," Michael called to her.

In the window of the shop, there was a photocopy of one of the pictures that Michael had in his briefcase. The flyer was titled MISSING WOMAN. Under the caption a thin-faced woman stared back. She had beautiful blond hair styled in a long bob, small features, and a reserved smile. Below the picture there was a brief description of Mary Chamblis: Five feet, five inches; 110 pounds, blond hair, brown eyes. "IF ANYONE HAS INFORMATION ABOUT THIS WOMAN, PLEASE CONTACT THE SHERIFF'S DEPARTMENT OR WYN DALTON." Telephone numbers were listed, along with the promise of an impressive reward for information.

"She's very thin, isn't she?" Elizabeth noted, studying the picture.

Michael shrugged. "Not everyone can be perfect like you."

"Stop it," she scolded. "We're discussing a serious matter."

"I'm very serious."

She looked up at him and smiled; then she turned back to the window. "Look at the display of items in the window over here." She pointed to another display on the opposite side of the door. There was a collection of corn shuck dolls, banjos, dulcimers, and various arrangements of dried flowers in attractive pottery.

"Come on," Elizabeth urged, hurrying ahead. "I can't wait to browse around."

Michael pressed the old-fashioned wooden latch, and they entered the shop. The scent of sweet cranberry mingled with the aroma of pine. Elizabeth took a deep breath, enjoying the smells as her eyes drifted around, spotting the soft glow of cranberry cake candles and baskets of fragrant pine soap. It was a wonderful touch.

Tall ceilings with skylights illuminated the many beautiful items on display, and the manner in which they were displayed was ingenious as well. Wooden islands grouped similar items together. This store far exceeded the usual arts-and-crafts store. Here there were original pieces of work that Elizabeth had not seen elsewhere. There were five-string fretted banjos with a pamphlet to explain their history and origin; there were dulcimers made of walnut and chestnut. Fascinated by the dulcimers,

Elizabeth stopped to read the brochure that proclaimed the dulcimer, like the banjo, to be an authentic American instrument. Glancing up at Michael, who was moving on, she read another sentence before replacing the brochure.

"Well, I've just learned something I never knew," she said as she caught up with Michael.

"And what is that?" he asked, trailing his hand over a polished oak rocking chair.

"The dulcimer is a combination of the Latin word *dulce* and the Greek word *melos,* and when you put those two words together it means 'a sweet song.'"

The next display that caught Elizabeth's eye was an interesting collection of gourds hanging at different eye levels to capture a customer's attention.

"Michael, what are these?" she asked, pointing. A pretty young woman stepped from behind the counter. "Maybe I can answer that." She was petite, obviously pregnant, and her face was one of natural beauty. Short brown blond hair framed delicate features in an oval face.

"Those are martin gourds," she explained. "They're handmade, of course, and their purpose is to entice the martins to come."

"Oh, I see. They're like little bird houses." Elizabeth examined one after another.

"Yes. Martins keep flying insects away from yards and gardens. Also, they're supposed to help keep mosquitoes and gnats away in the summer."

Michael was studying the gourds. "I think I remember Mom and Dad having some of these out in the garden when I was a kid."

"My grandmother wouldn't think of not having several gourds around her yard and garden." The young woman's face lit up with a smile as her brown eyes moved from Michael to Elizabeth.

"Incidentally, I'm Laurel Wentworth." She offered her hand.

"Hi," Michael and Elizabeth replied in unison.

Michael took the initiative. "I'm Michael Calloway, and this is my wife, Elizabeth."

"Nice to meet both of you." She shook their hands, looking from one to the other. "I've been so excited about meeting a top-notch detective and a Christian psychologist! What a team you two must make." Laurel's eyes twinkled.

Elizabeth laughed and looked at Michael. "Well, sometimes we have our differences, but, yes," she sighed, as her hand slipped into his, "I think we're a good team." She looked back at Laurel. "I met your friend Jessica Vandercamp at Seascape."

"Jessica!" Laurel exclaimed. "How is she?"

"Very happy," Elizabeth replied. "She told me what a wonderful shop you have, and I'm dying to look around—"

"But first," Michael interrupted gently, "I'd like to speak with Matt. Then you can shop to your heart's content, darling." He winked at Elizabeth.

A look of regret crossed Laurel's face. "I'm sorry, but Matt's gone into Atlanta on business. He'll be back tomorrow. If it's about the Chamblis woman, I would suggest you go down to the end of the street and talk with the sheriff. He's been investigating." She paused, looking thoughtful. "It's a shame that she is still missing after such a thorough search. I understand her fiancé is really distraught."

"Yes, he's the one who hired us," Michael explained. "I've only spoken with him over the phone at his office in Knoxville, but he's driving up to meet with us once we get settled."

"By the way," Elizabeth intervened, "could you recommend a place for us to stay? We'd like something small and cozy." She looked from Michael to Laurel. "Maybe one of those chalets with a fireplace like I've seen advertised."

Laurel nodded and smiled again. "There are lots of nice places around Gatlinburg and Pigeon Forge, but if you want to stay here, I know a special place. It was just built last year, but it's quaint, nice, and comfortable. You'll even have a mountain stream outside your window." She smiled at Elizabeth. "It's called Windwhispers."

"Sounds romantic." Elizabeth turned to Michael with a smile. "What do you think?"

"Sounds perfect to me," he agreed, looking back at Laurel. "We certainly appreciate your recommending it."

"Glad to help. If you'd like, I'll call Mrs. Foster now and see if she has a chalet available."

"That would be great. Thanks, Laurel," Elizabeth replied, then tilted her eyes up at Michael. They were looking forward to spending some time alone. There hadn't been much chance for privacy since she had recovered her memory and testified in the trial. Then, Katie had been all over them, along with family and even the press.

While Laurel telephoned the owner of the chalet, Michael glanced into Elizabeth's uptilted face and felt an urge to kiss her, a habit that was occurring whenever the opportunity presented itself. But that could wait, he decided, noticing the other customers mingling around the shop.

Laurel had been talking to Mrs. Foster on the telephone, but now she put her on hold and turned to face them. "She wants to know if you're wanting to go on out there now."

Michael and Elizabeth exchanged glances, and Michael nodded. "Yes, I think we'd like to get settled, Laurel. Will we have a phone out there?"

"Oh, yes." Laurel smiled. "And fortunately for you, there

was a cancellation an hour ago, so you two can get a chalet."

"What luck," Elizabeth said as she looked from Laurel to Michael.

While Laurel confirmed their reservations, Elizabeth turned to take another look at the jewelry. Within the glass counters a variety of silver bracelets and rings nestled on beds of black velvet.

"All right, darling, go on and pick out something," Michael said, knowing his wife was eager to get a closer look at some of the jewelry on display inside the glass counter.

"Just one something?" Elizabeth teased, her eyes moving from one item to another.

Michael grinned at her, knowing there was nothing he could deny her now. Furthermore, their finances were in good shape, so why not splurge? "Pick out whatever you want," he said.

Elizabeth stood on tiptoe to plant a kiss on his cheek before she eagerly turned to the display case.

"I have an idea," Michael suggested. "Why don't you stay here and look around while I walk down and talk with the sheriff about Mary Chamblis?"

"Great!" Elizabeth nodded, still staring wide-eyed at the treasures.

"Be back in half an hour," Michael whispered in her ear, trying to be sure she had understood him.

She turned her head to face him as a wide smile lit her face. "Take your time, darling. I'll be right here."

Michael nodded and smiled at Laurel. She smiled back over the head of a customer who had come to her with a question. She waved as he walked through the front door and stepped onto the sidewalk.

Autumn was coming early to the area, and he was glad.

Pumpkins of all sizes and shapes provided colorful displays in shop windows, on the porches of restaurants, and in the yard of a quaint little house. He lifted his nose, absorbing the wonderful aroma of cinnamon and spice from the apple-dumpling shop he was passing. Wood smoke from chimney fires floated on the crisp breeze, and again he felt as though he were drifting back in time and space.

He thrust his hands into the pockets of his jeans and strolled on to the end of the block where the police department was located. Within, he quickly found the sheriff's office.

A little man wearing a navy uniform with a deputy's badge stepped forward.

"Can I help you?"

Michael chewed the inside of his lip to hold back a chuckle. For a moment he felt as if he had just landed in the center of Mayberry and was facing Barney. Of course, this man was not Barney; he just bore a striking resemblance in every way: his stature, his thin, angular face, even the way he seemed to wear his importance like another badge.

"I'm Michael Calloway," he said as he removed a business card from his billfold and handed it to the deputy. "I own a detective agency in Atlanta. I've been employed by Wyn Dalton to try to help locate his fiancée, Mary Chamblis."

"Is that right?" The man's eyes widened as he read the card. "You're from Atlanta? Well, I'll be. Oh, I'm Jasper Colburn," he said, extending a hand.

"Is the sheriff in?" Michael asked, looking around the small cluttered office.

"Nope. He's gone over to Gatlinburg, but—" he pressed his chest forward—"I'm in charge. Can I help you?"

"I hope so. Have you had any leads on Mary Chamblis?"

Jasper gave a wag of his head, which Michael interpreted as

a no. "Frankly, I think she fell off one of those steep trails around Painted Rock."

"Oh, really?" Michael studied him curiously. "Then why hasn't she been located? I understand you guys have conducted a good search."

Jasper nodded. "Search-and-rescue combed the area on foot and by helicopter. Problem is—" Jasper raked through his thin brown hair—"there's so many deep hollows, places she could have fallen and—" He broke off, frowning.

"And what?"

Jasper folded his arms over his chest. "Well, there's some pretty mean bears back up in those hollows. Especially the ones with cubs."

"Wouldn't the searchers have found some of her clothing?"

Jasper shook his head. "Not if a bear carried her off to its den."

Michael considered that for only a moment, then pressed on. "What about the possibility that she was abducted?"

Jasper shook his head. "There hasn't been a ransom call."

Michael nodded. He had already discussed this with Wyn Dalton. Wyn was prepared to pay a ransom and had gone home to wait for a call that never came. Now he was offering a reward for information.

"What's your theory of the old-model van that was seen out at Painted Rock near the time of Mary's disappearance?" he asked Jasper, watching his reaction.

"We already checked those folks out," Jasper asserted proudly. "They're just some blue-collar workers from Birmingham, Alabama. Harmless, but a little strange."

"What do you mean by *strange?*"

Jasper shrugged. "A couple in their late twenties who seem like modern-day hippies. The sheriff's still keeping tabs on them," Jasper inserted, obviously feeling that he needed a little more authority to convince Michael.

"Do you have some information on them?" Michael asked.

"Sure do." He turned and headed toward a thick file on his desk, flipping awkwardly through the contents. "What's it like being a detective down in Atlanta?" Jasper eyed him with curiosity.

Michael sighed. "It's pretty hectic. I'd rather be tracking people down in this kind of setting."

"Don't reckon you've been up some of these coves yet," Jasper snorted, looking back to the folder. "We've got some curious folks back up in these hills. They don't take to strangers, so be careful. Here you are." He withdrew several pages of notes, then hesitated. "You know, I'd better wait and let Sheriff Grayson handle this. I can't go giving out privileged information."

Michael suppressed a sigh. "Okay, I'll check back with Sheriff Grayson. When do you expect him?"

Jasper straightened, closing the file. "He'll be here tomorrow. I don't want to seem unfriendly...." Jasper looked troubled.

"You're just being a good deputy," Michael said with a smile. "Besides, my wife and I need to get settled. In fact—" he glanced at his watch—"I left her shopping down at the Wentworths' store."

"Uh-oh." Jasper's eyes widened. "She could buy a lot of stuff in there."

Michael nodded. "And she probably will. Incidentally, we'll be staying out at Windwhispers if you need to reach us."

"So you're gonna stay out near Painted Rock, huh?"

"Do you think those chalets are okay?"

"Oh sure." Jasper grinned. "I guess you want to be near the site of the disappearance."

Michael smiled back, indulging him. "Sometimes it's helpful. Strangers have a way of picking up things local people take for granted."

Jasper's eyebrows hiked, as though he was wondering if this was some sort of personal criticism of the law here.

"What I mean is, when other detectives come into my area, they have a fresh perspective, sometimes see something I've taken for granted."

"Hmm." Jasper's gray eyes widened. "Reckon that makes sense. Well, I'll tell Sheriff Grayson that you're here."

"Thanks." Michael extended his hand. "Nice meeting you, Jasper."

"Likewise." Jasper nodded, trying to pull off an act of sophistication that was less than convincing.

When Michael returned to the shop, he found Elizabeth engaged in deep conversation with Laurel. A beautiful handmade quilt and a small silver ring were lying on the counter beside her purse. If these were her only purchases, he could breathe a sigh of relief. He knew how Elizabeth loved to shop.

"Oh, hi, darling." Elizabeth whirled to greet him, slipping a hand through his arm. "I want you to see this amazing quilt made by a Cherokee lady. Isn't it beautiful?"

Michael studied the design of a white rose with a gold center and seven green leaves artfully woven onto the stem.

"Let me explain it to you." Elizabeth was trailing her fingers gently over the soft quilt. "This is the Cherokee rose from the Trail of Tears. There is a legend that when the Cherokees were sent on the Trail of Tears in 1838, the elders prayed for a sign to lift their spirits. Mothers were grieving over losing husbands and children. Along the trail they started finding this beautiful rose." Elizabeth indicated the rose on the quilt. "Supposedly the rose represented the tears the women shed. The wild

Cherokee rose can be seen along that trail even today."

Michael nodded, gently touching the soft quilt. "That's a touching story. And I like the quilt."

"And do you like this? It's for Katie." Elizabeth lifted a small silver ring that gleamed in the palm of her hand.

"Perfect," Michael grinned. "What about something for you?"

"Just the quilt and the ring for now."

"Aha." Michael grinned, looking from Elizabeth to Laurel, who was approaching them. "You caught that, didn't you, Laurel? She plans on another visit here."

"Good. I want her to come back. And I was just extending an invitation for dinner to you two. Since today is Wednesday, I can assure you that by Friday evening Matt will be back and we'll be ready for company. Could you come?"

Elizabeth looked at Michael. "I'd love it, unless you've already made plans for us."

"I haven't made plans. Dinner on Friday evening is fine with me. Thanks, Laurel. I'm looking forward to talking with Matt."

"And he wants to see you."

Elizabeth had already paid for her purchases, and now Laurel was wrapping them. Elizabeth turned to Michael. "Darling, Laurel has met Mary Chamblis. She's been in the shop, and we were just discussing her."

"Oh?"

Elizabeth nodded. "Laurel, will you please tell Michael what you told me about Mary Chamblis?"

Laurel handed the package to Elizabeth and looked at Michael. "The couple were in here a couple of times this past summer. As I told Elizabeth, it's just my own judgment, but she seemed like a woman who was strangely preoccupied. I don't know any other way to put it. She kept looking at all the crafts, and she asked a lot of questions about the area. But when I asked about her life, she clammed up. That's not unusual. Some people, particularly those who are connected to wealthy families as she was, don't say much about their lives. They've learned it's best not to do that. So she wasn't a woman who went around letting people know that her fiancé's family could pay a hefty ransom." Laurel sighed. "And yet it seems someone must have figured that out."

"What did you think of Wyn Dalton?" Michael asked.

"We never really talked. He was looking around too, but he seemed nice enough. Matt talked with him more than I. After Mary disappeared, he was in and out of the shop, asking everyone questions."

Michael nodded. "Do you remember when they were here together?"

"Yes, I already checked on that for the sheriff. They were here over Memorial Day weekend and again during the Fourth of July. We were swamped, but I remember her because of the charge card. I saw her name, and later when the posters went up around town with her face, I knew she had been in the shop. I went back through the credit-card slips and found her name and the dates I just mentioned."

Elizabeth and Michael listened thoughtfully for a moment. "Just out of curiosity, what did Mary Chamblis buy?" Elizabeth asked.

Laurel hesitated. "She liked so many things. The credit slip indicated she purchased several small items, but the specific ones weren't listed." She shook her head. "I wish I could be of more help."

"You've already helped." Elizabeth smiled at her, then looked at Michael.

"Yes, thanks a lot."

"She's told me where to find their place when we go for dinner on Friday evening," Elizabeth said. "It's that gorgeous home on the edge of town just as we came in."

"Then we'll be looking forward to visiting with you and Matt," Michael said. "What can we bring?"

She shook her head. "Nothing. Just be prepared for a busy little two-year-old who never runs down."

Elizabeth laughed. "We have a daughter who was a caricature of the terrible twos at that age, so believe me, we learned patience years ago."

Laughing, they said good-bye and headed out of the store with their purchases and Laurel's directions for Windwhispers.

Once they were comfortably seated in the Blazer and heading west, Elizabeth turned to Michael. "What did you find out at the sheriff's office?"

He chuckled. "The sheriff was over in Gatlinburg, and the man in charge is the perfect model for Barney in Mayberry."

"You're kidding." Elizabeth grinned.

"No, I'm serious. I tried to concentrate on what Jasper Colburn—that's the name of the deputy—was saying, but I kept thinking about Barney on that TV show. The upshot was, he assumes Mary Chamblis fell into one of those coves and a bear dragged her off to his den."

Elizabeth's eyes widened in horror as a hand shot up to her mouth. "Oh no! How terrible."

"How convenient in solving the mystery," Michael said wryly. "I don't really buy that, although I'm not a native here, so I have to respect their opinion. He says the search-and-rescue unit has covered the valleys and coves and can find no trace of her. Something Jasper said did snag my interest, though. He made a reference to some of the people up in the coves being unfriendly to strangers, behaving curiously. It's possible that she may be staying in some old mountaineer's cabin—against her will."

"Do you really think that's possible?" Elizabeth asked gravely. "This *is* the twentieth century, you know."

"Right now, it's the most logical thing I've heard. Remind me to call Wyn Dalton as soon as we get checked in. I want to make an appointment to see him as soon as possible and get his feedback on what may have happened. I'm anxious to hear his side of the story."

"It will be interesting to learn just what his viewpoint is on this." She leaned her head back against the seat and watched the brilliant display of colors unfold before them. The rich green hillsides they had seen on their previous trip were now turning to luminous golds and crimsons and oranges as the Blazer wound its way up the mountain to the small wooden sign indicating the turnoff to Windwhispers.

"Oh look, Michael. This is wonderful." Elizabeth was pointing toward the Swiss-style chalets that were spaced every quarter mile along the road winding up to the rental office. Behind the cabins was a twisting little stream that glinted silver in the afternoon sunshine. The setting was postcard perfect.

While Michael went to the office to check in, Elizabeth stretched her legs and looked out over the panoramic view.

"Oh, God, how great thou art," she said, taking in the rolling mountains, the rich green spruce and pine, the bursts of orange and gold and flaming red in the oaks and maples, and the mist-filled valley below. The setting was more beautiful than any painting Elizabeth had ever seen, but then only God could paint such a portrait, she thought, awed by the beauty before her.

"Like it?" She heard Michael's soft voice just above her ear as his arms wound around her waist.

"I love it," she sighed, turning in his arms. "Did you get our chalet?"

He dangled the key and grinned, and she followed him back to the Blazer.

Their chalet featured a wide deck across the front, offering a spectacular view. Inside they wandered through the living room, complete with stone fireplace, rocking chairs, and picturesque views through the spacious glass windows. There was a small dining area with a cozy table and chairs, and the kitchen was completely furnished with utensils, dishes, and a coffeemaker. The bedroom featured a queen-size bed with a fluffy comforter and plump white pillows.

"Looks too pretty to sleep in," Michael commented while Elizabeth peered into the adjoining bath.

"And in here we have a Jacuzzi." She turned back to Michael, her eyes gleaming with mischief.

He grinned, taking her into his arms. "Then what are we waiting for?"

TWO

The phone interrupted their afternoon nap, and Michael stirred sleepily in the bed. Elizabeth, snuggled against his side, scarcely moved.

Carefully he reached for the phone on the bedside table, trying not to disturb Elizabeth. He managed to sound reasonably awake as he breathed a hello into the phone. He had phoned Wyn Dalton's office earlier, leaving the number where they could be reached.

"Michael Calloway?" The male voice sounded uncertain.

"Speaking."

"Oh, hello. This is Wyn Dalton. How was your trip?"

"We had a good trip, and now we're enjoying the scenery. I'm anxious to meet with you. When would that be convenient?"

"I was hoping we could have dinner tonight," Wyn replied. "I'm planning to leave the office early and can meet you in a couple of hours."

Michael peered at his watch. "That would be around six?"

"Yes, at six. There's a good restaurant between Angel Valley and Gatlinburg." He gave the name and location, and Michael nodded in response.

"Yes, I remember passing it on the way. We'll meet you at six, then."

"Looking forward to it," Wyn Dalton said before he hung up.

Elizabeth stirred sleepily. "Who was that?"

"Our employer, darling." He leaned over to plant a kiss on her parted lips. "Wake up and shine. We have a missing woman to locate!"

Wyn Dalton was smaller than Michael by several inches, and comparing Wyn's height to his own, Michael judged him to be about five feet, ten inches. With light brown hair and pale blue eyes, his face looked younger than Michael had pictured from their phone conversations. Either life had been easy for him or he merely looked young for his age. Mary Chamblis was twenty-two, but Michael had assumed that the president of Dalton Chemicals would be at least thirty. This guy didn't look a day over twenty-six.

Wyn was wearing a neat navy blazer over tan slacks, with a tan T-shirt underneath. His clothes were well designed and expensively trendy. Watching Wyn's eyes sweep over Michael's casual tan khakis and long-sleeved blue cotton shirt, Michael wondered if he should have topped his shirt with a jacket as well. He quickly dismissed the idea. His wardrobe was not as important as his competence, and for once, he was going to do his job without a suit and tie, in a relaxed setting.

Wyn's eyes moved on to Elizabeth. She was wearing a pale blue cotton turtleneck with matching cotton skirt that stretched to her navy ankle boots. Her straight blond hair swept her shoulders, framing her soft brown eyes and delicate face.

"I'm Wyn Dalton," he said, shaking hands, first with Michael and then Elizabeth.

He was waiting for them in the foyer of the casually elegant restaurant. "I already have a table for us."

He turned to the hostess and nodded, and she led them around linen-covered tables where the glow of candles illuminated the gleaming silver and sparkling china.

After winding past several couples, a few singles, and one family, they were finally seated at a table in the corner, roomy yet secluded, near a fireplace that stretched halfway across the wall. Huge logs filled the fireplace, where a low fire added to the coziness of the setting.

Michael held Elizabeth's chair and then took a seat opposite Wyn. Crystal goblets were quickly filled with ice water and menus distributed.

"I'd like to recommend the Filet Oscar," Wyn said, without opening the menu. "If you like steak, I think theirs is the very best."

"Mmm," Michael said and looked at Elizabeth. "Sounds good to me."

Elizabeth studied the menu. "I think I'd rather go with something lighter. Perhaps the chicken fettuccine."

Wyn stared at her for a moment, then dropped his eyes. "Mary always ordered that."

Elizabeth's head jerked up. "Oh...." She glanced at Michael, wondering if she should apologize for her choice of food, but then it was Wyn who spoke again.

"I'm sorry. The memories just keep nagging at me. You'll enjoy that particular dish," he said, looking sad. Then his eyes moved on to Michael. "And their salads are always fresh. Would you like an appetizer? Or perhaps a bottle of Chablis?"

They both shook their heads. "No, we'll just wait for the food."

"Then we've decided," Wyn said, nodding at the server, who instantly stepped forward to swoop up their menus and stand at attention for their orders. Wyn smoothly gave the orders, inquiring as to how Michael wanted his steak, what kind of dressing Elizabeth preferred, and then their preference for sweetened or unsweetened tea, once they had ordered. He was the perfect host. The server stood silent, allowing Wyn to do his job for him.

As Wyn spoke, Elizabeth was struck by how smooth he was, how adeptly he handled servers, guests, and food selections. *Born with the silver spoon in his mouth*, her grandmother would have said.

"Well." He folded his hands on the table and looked at Michael after the server had disappeared. "I guess you'd like my version of the last time I saw Mary," he said, taking a deep breath.

"Even though we discussed it over the phone," Michael answered, "I'd like to hear it again if you don't mind. I may have a couple of questions."

Wyn's eyes swept Michael's face, and he nodded. "I've told it so many times that I could recite it in my sleep," he said, trying to dredge up some humor but failing. "Mary enjoyed driving up to the Smokies, and so did I. Both of us were tired from a long, draining week at the office, and we needed a break. Mary worked in our accounting department, and I must admit we've suffered since her absence."

He sighed and began again. "It was Saturday morning, and we had already decided to spend the weekend up here. We left Knoxville around eight, stopped for brunch along the way, then drove on toward Painted Rock. After being cooped up at Dalton Chemicals all week, we wanted to get out and do some hiking. We had packed snacks and a thermos of coffee for the afternoon."

He stopped talking while the server appeared with iced tea, a basket of bread wrapped in a white linen cloth, and then plates of crisp salad. Everything was exactly as they had ordered. It was obvious to Michael that the server knew Wyn and was accustomed to being prompt with his food.

Wyn reached for the basket of rolls, passing the basket first to Elizabeth, then to Michael. Without saying a word to interrupt the story, they each took a roll, quietly buttered it, and continued to pay attention to Wyn, who himself seemed uninterested in the bread.

"When we got to the base of Painted Rock, we parked in the designated parking area." He hesitated for a moment, taking a sip of tea and staring into the candlelight. "We got out, and I locked the car. I wanted to visit the men's facilities nearby. The last time I saw Mary, she was walking toward a lookout at the base of the mountain." He dropped his eyes, staring at his hands, still folded on the table. "When I came out of the restroom and went to the head of the trail, she was nowhere in sight."

He took a deep breath and looked at his salad for a moment, then halfheartedly picked up his fork. "I sat down and waited, thinking nothing about it for the first fifteen minutes or so. Then I remembered there had been a white van parked about ten yards from us when we arrived. It was an old van—I don't know what year; the police have already asked—just an old, beat-up white van with Alabama license plates. The reason I remember the state is because Mary mentioned something about wanting to go down to Gulf Shores in southern Alabama."

"But the sheriff did track down the van?"

Wyn nodded, chewing his salad slowly. "Fortunately an older couple noticed the van that day and gave the sheriff a better description. I just remember glancing into the front seat and seeing a couple, both rather shabby looking. There were curtains across the back windows, so I don't know what was back there. Later I learned from the sheriff that the couple was Leon and Ruth Ann Fisher."

Michael was listening intently, trying to picture the scene exactly as it had transpired. "When you came out of the restroom, the van was gone?"

"That's right. And Mary was nowhere in sight. Halfway up the trail I saw a middle-aged man and woman with a boy about thirteen—the Todd Blankenship family, I later learned—returning from the top of Painted Rock. I asked them if they had seen a slim blond woman on the trail. They said they hadn't."

"Were those the only people around?" Michael asked. "I would have thought on a Saturday—"

"There were people up at the top, and a few others hiking on various trails. But I questioned everyone, even took down their names. After that, the sheriff and his staff claim to have requestioned those people, along with everyone else in the area. Nobody recalls seeing Mary." A frown marred Wyn's high forehead, and Michael decided maybe Wyn was twenty-seven. "The problem is, there are so many hiking trails in these mountains that it's easy to get lost."

"But why would Mary wander off?" Elizabeth asked, unable to stem her curiosity.

Wyn looked at Elizabeth as though analyzing her reason for the question. "I don't know. I've asked myself that a hundred times. She loved walking the trails. She might have spotted a certain kind of flower that she wanted to get a better look at. I think she'd like to have been an artist. Actually, she tried once but then gave up. Felt she didn't have the talent."

They were now into their entrees, and still Wyn's appetite had not picked up. Michael and Elizabeth dug in heartily, unable to restrain their voracious appetites, stimulated by the mountain air and a light lunch.

Wyn fell silent, cutting his steak carefully, precisely; then he glanced at Michael. "After you called saying you and your wife had planned a trip to Angel Valley and you'd like a crack at the case, I checked you out." He grinned wryly, although he did not seem embarrassed to admit he had investigated Michael. "You have a good reputation for finding missing people. I'm hoping you can find Mary."

Michael nodded. "I'll do my best. Is there anything else that you can tell me? I gather the search-and-rescue team made an all-out effort."

He shrugged. "They said they did, and I can't prove they didn't."

"Does that mean you doubt them?"

He sighed and pushed his plate away. "I don't know what I mean. They keep talking about all the coves and back country. I realize there's an enormous amount of ground to cover if...she fell."

Michael shook his head. "I just have the feeling that if she had fallen, she would have screamed, and someone would have heard her. I don't see how that could have gone unnoticed."

Wyn turned his head and looked at him rather curiously. "Funny, you're the first person to see it that way. But then, that's why I hired you. I'm counting on you to find what the others have missed. I thought she might have taken a side trail and then become lost. If she's still out there somewhere, I imagine she's slightly disoriented and won't make too much sense at first."

Michael nodded, although he wasn't sure about that. The presence of the van continued to nag at his thoughts. "About that van," Michael said. "I want to check out the people who were inside that day."

"Please do." Wyn looked encouraged.

"Excuse me," Elizabeth interrupted gently, "but why haven't

you been notified if someone abducted her?"

Wyn's pale blue eyes grew cynical. "That's everybody's question. Especially mine. Mary's been gone for three and a half weeks now. After I waited around here for a day and night, the sheriff suggested I return to my home and wait for a phone call. As I told you over the phone, the call never came."

"Where did Mary live?" Elizabeth asked.

"She lived in a condo a few blocks from me. I have a key to her apartment, and I went there first thing. Everything was just as it was when we left that morning. Nobody had been there; nothing had been disturbed. And it's the very same way now."

"This is really puzzling," Elizabeth said, looking from Wyn to Michael. "But you have a real pro on the job now," she added, smiling at her husband. "He's a stickler for details that other people miss. I believe Michael will find her," she said confidently.

Wyn Dalton studied her thoughtfully for a moment before his eyes swung back to Michael. "I'm counting on that. Funny thing was, whenever Mary looked out at the mist in the valleys, she said it made her think of spirits. It almost seems as if those spirits she believed in swallowed her up," he said gravely, staring into space for a moment.

"I don't believe in misty spirits, Wyn," Michael quickly answered. "I'll be looking for a real abductor; I can assure you of that."

Wyn gave a half smile of hope, then glanced at his watch. "Well, it's after eight, and I have a long drive back to the city. You have all of my numbers, don't you?"

Michael removed the small notebook he carried in his shirt pocket and flipped it open to the first page. "Home phone, office phone, fax machine, e-mail, cell phone. I don't think I'll have a problem getting in touch with you." He grinned as he closed his notebook and returned it to his shirt pocket.

Wyn nodded. "Then you two take your time with the meal, stay as long as you like." He picked up the tab. "It was nice meeting you," he said looking from one to the another, "and I'll call you tomorrow."

They said their good-byes, and Michael and Elizabeth both stared after him as he left the dining room. He walked with the brisk, purposeful stride of a businessman, never glancing back at them, pushing through the door and bumping a couple, yet hurrying on with only a brief apology.

"What do you think?" Michael turned to Elizabeth.

She hesitated, took a long sip of tea, then placed the glass carefully on the table. "He seems like a nice guy, worried, concerned, and…rich. It shows in every way."

"So you don't see a reason for her taking off on her own?"

Elizabeth's eyes widened. "The thought never occurred to me."

"That's always a possibility in a case like this. Remember how Jackie DeRidder appeared to go missing, yet she did the unpredictable and left on her own."

"There's quite a difference in Jackie DeRidder and what we know of Mary Chamblis," Elizabeth reminded him.

Michael nodded. "I did a background check on Mary, and there seems to be no reason for her to take off. She came from a very modest background. Her father had worked for Dalton Chemicals for years. She was coming into money for the first time in her life, and apparently there was no problem between her and Wyn's family. They paid her tuition for a two-year business course. The wedding was already planned; she had selected her china and crystal, all those things that brides do." He shrugged. "There just doesn't seem to be a reason for her vanishing act."

Elizabeth nodded in agreement. "What is the sheriff's theory?"

"I'll be interested in hearing that in the morning. He was in Gatlinburg today," Michael reminded her. "So—" he glanced at their empty plates—"do we have dessert, or do we go?"

She pressed a hand to her stomach and laughed. "We go while I can still walk." She glanced at her empty plate. "That was delicious. It's so good to be able to enjoy food again, Michael."

He smiled and reached across the table for her hand. "I knew exactly how Wyn felt when he was picking over his food. I lost ten pounds while you were sick, and you lost even more."

"Well—" she placed her napkin on the table and stood— "that's all in the past. Let's help this poor guy and Mary find each other again."

He nodded and reached for her hand as they strolled from the restaurant, grateful that they were together again…forever.

Sheriff Grayson was a sturdy, no-nonsense guy whom Michael decided might have spent his early years in a boxing ring. He was just under six feet, yet his body looked strong and firm despite the gray hair on his head. Lines cut across his forehead and down his cheek, and his nose was a bit crooked, as though it had been broken at one time or another. Still, his reserved smile appeared genuine.

"What's my theory?" Sheriff Grayson repeated Michael's question as they sipped coffee from Styrofoam mugs, compliments of the small office. "I think she wandered off for one reason or another, fell, and we haven't located her. There seems to be no other explanation."

Michael nodded. "It would appear that way. But why didn't

someone hear her scream when she fell?"

"Because there were some kids on a field trip at the top of Painted Rock. They were making enough noise to drown out almost anything."

"But the people who were returning along the trail?"

He shrugged. "They could have been talking; they could have mistaken her scream for that of a wild animal. Ever hear the wail of a coyote? Or someone simply abducted her for their own selfish reasons and doesn't want a ransom."

Michael took a sip of coffee, analyzing those suggestions. Another possibility occurred to him. "Jasper mentioned there are some deep coves where folks are not too friendly. Is it possible that she could have somehow ended up in a mountaineer's cabin?"

"Quite possible," Sheriff Grayson agreed, looking across at Michael with clear hazel eyes. "And it's hard to find every cabin, but we've done our best. So far we haven't turned up anything, but maybe you'll come across some place we've overlooked."

"I wish I could, but I'm sure you've done a thorough job. You know this area a lot better than I do."

"If we can be of help, let us know. We're still investigating."

Michael hesitated, remembering something. "Oh, there is one more thing. The people in the old van from Birmingham."

The Sheriff shrugged. "We always come back to that too. But we can't find anything on the Fishers, and they swear they saw the couple together just before they drove away."

Sheriff Grayson opened the thick file. "Jasper said you were interested in them, so I've had Lucy make a copy of the notes I have. You're welcome to check them out yourself, although they've gone back to Alabama."

He handed Michael three pages of notes. "I frankly think

they're telling the truth. They saw Wyn and Mary drive up and get out, but the Fishers claim to have driven off right afterward. They say they have no idea what happened to her. I ran both Leon and Ruth Fisher through the computer; there's nothing on them. They're blue-collar workers by week, and they devote their weekends to camping when they have some spare time. No children." He handed Michael copies of his notes and volunteered no more information. He merely sipped his coffee, studying Michael over the cup.

Michael checked the pages in his hand. There was a photograph of the couple, who looked to be in their late twenties. The man had shoulder-length brown hair and matching beard. There was a hole in the knee of his jeans and his flannel shirt looked worn. The woman beside him seemed to be a softer version of the man—straggly brown hair, narrow-set eyes and a small, crooked smile. She, too, was wearing worn-looking clothes, jeans and a T-shirt. They appeared to live on the fringes of poverty, and there was nothing malicious in their eyes, but Michael knew from experience that one could not draw conclusions from appearances.

He glanced over the fact sheet: The guy was twenty-eight, the girl twenty-six, and their address was North Bender, Bessemer, Alabama, a suburb of Birmingham. His trade was carpenter, and she was a housecleaner.

"What feeling did you get while interviewing these people, Sheriff?" Michael glanced back at the man who looked as though he would hit the mark on sizing people up.

"From everything I can turn up on them, they're harmless," he replied. "In the beginning, of course, they were our prime suspects, but we located them and questioned them for hours. Their story is that they pulled over, hiked down the west trail a mile or so, shared a picnic lunch and made some pictures, then returned to their van and drove off."

Michael nodded, tapping the report against his thumb. "Where does that west trail lead?"

"About a quarter of a mile down, it forks. The main trail leads to the right and eventually runs back into a wider trail going up to the top of Painted Rock. The other trail just runs off into the woods, and we found no sign of her there."

"What about footprints?" Michael inquired.

"Fall leaves and grass cover the trail, and then there was a rain that night. The rain left the ground muddy in places, and we could have tracked someone if the rain had come earlier. But the ground was dry that afternoon. We never found any footprints leading down either trail. But, like I said, leaves and pine needles were thick, and that would conceal footprints."

Michael nodded and sighed. "Every lead seems to have been followed." He chewed his lip and thought about it. "How far did you follow both trails?"

The sheriff looked surprised for the first time, tipping Michael off that the trail had not been pursued completely. "We followed the main trail all the way to the top of Painted Rock. The more obscure trail we followed for over a mile. Didn't seem to make sense that she'd be wandering further than that with her boyfriend waiting for her. And besides, there are signs on the trails warning of bears and wild game."

Michael nodded. That made sense to him, too.

"Well." He tucked the report inside the briefcase he had brought with him today. "I don't know how I can improve on what you guys have already done."

The statement was made to stay in the sheriff's good graces although Michael had to admit the report seemed to be thorough. And yet Michael knew that many times the obvious was overlooked by locals, where an outside detective might pick up on something that had been missed.

He extended his hand. "It's been a pleasure meeting you, sir." He handed him a business card on which he had already inked in the number of the chalet where they were staying.

"I'd appreciate it if you could keep me informed."

"I'll do that. You comfortable out at Windwhispers?"

Michael grinned. "Best night's sleep I've had in a long time. What a relief to be out of that Atlanta traffic."

The sheriff chuckled. "That's what they all say. Well, good luck, and be sure to keep us informed if you turn up anything."

"I will," Michael agreed, walking to the door. "See you later."

As he drove back to the chalet to pick up Elizabeth, who was getting another hour of sleep, Michael realized the next most-important thing to do was go to Painted Rock and have a look around. If Elizabeth wanted to tag along, they could stop at the service station and food mart next door and pick up some snacks to take with them.

Once he arrived back at their chalet, he found Elizabeth showered and ready to go. She wore jeans, and a heavy sweater that resembled his own, only his was blue, and hers was red.

"Are we trying to be the Bobsey twins?" he asked, his eyes moving from her tennis shoes to his own.

"Nope. This just appealed to me for a day of hiking. If my instincts are right, we're going to Painted Rock, aren't we?"

He chuckled. "Your instincts are right, as usual. Only we need to throw our hiking boots in the Blazer. That is, if you're up to a long hike."

"I'm as physically fit as you are, Michael Calloway," she teased, as they shared a mischievous look.

He grinned. "No time for the Jacuzzi?"

"Not till we come back," she smiled playfully, grabbing her thermal jacket.

That prompted him to reach for his jacket. "Then we're off."

An hour later, after stopping at several lookout points, scanning the valley, and talking, they arrived at Painted Rock.

They locked the Blazer and set off along the main trail to get a look at the valley from the top. At first the trail veered gently upward, then it sharpened, growing more steep.

"Whew," Elizabeth sighed. "I'm out of shape."

"Wonder why I'm not winded yet?" Michael teased.

"Because you get up at five to run a mile every day. Please don't remind me." She had begun to pant, so she decided to conserve her energy and refrain from conversation. After another quarter mile they were looking across at mile-high mountains with hillsides of colorful trees spread before them like an artist's palette. Vast open meadows stretched back into deep coves, and as Michael looked through his binoculars, he realized there were many, many places where Mary could be held captive. It was a huge area to cover, and he didn't see how the search-and-rescue unit could possibly have explored all the nooks and crannies.

He pulled the binoculars down and looked at Elizabeth. Seeing the look of rapture on her face, he realized she was enjoying the view without thinking about Mary. He didn't want to spoil the moment for her, so he didn't voice his thoughts.

She turned to him and smiled. "I've always wanted to stand on top of the world and give you a big kiss."

Michael extended his arms. "I'd say this is the place."

Laughing, she nestled into his arms, and they kissed long and passionately; then Elizabeth pulled back, breathless. "I don't want to distract you from the search you're conducting here. We're supposed to be thinking about Mary Chamblis, aren't we?"

He took a deep breath, shaking himself back to the present. "Yeah, afraid so. But I don't think we're being disrespectful to our client to at least appreciate the view. And we'll come back again when we're free just to enjoy ourselves without worrying about the detective work. How does that sound to you?"

"Sounds wonderful. And maybe we can bring Katie."

He nodded. "Yeah, Katie would love it here. We could go over to Gatlinburg and ride horses. Wouldn't she be thrilled with that?"

"Stop it," Elizabeth scolded. "You're going to make me want to distract you from your job and nag you to go horseback riding."

"Won't do any good," Michael sighed, looking out at the view. "If she's out there, I'm going to find her. This is the kind of challenge that gets my adrenaline going."

"I know." Elizabeth turned again to scan the vast mountainscape. Then she looked back at Michael and shook her head. "Michael, how on earth are you going to find her?"

He sighed. "Honestly…I don't know. But we're not getting any closer here. Let's head back down to the base of the trail."

They turned and started back, holding hands until the trail narrowed and they had to walk single file. A light wind was whipping down from the mountainside, and a few clouds had begun to gather by the time they arrived back at the starting point.

"Looks like we made it just in time," Michael said as he unlocked the door and they sank gratefully into the front seat.

Elizabeth opened the sack and pulled out boxed sandwiches and bottled juice. They ate quickly and in silence, each momentarily lost in his or her own thoughts.

"I have an idea," Elizabeth said as she finished her sandwich and wiped her hands. "Let's replay the scene. You be Wyn and I'm Mary."

"Don't go falling off a mountain ledge or disappearing on me," Michael warned as he drained the carton of juice and placed their empty containers in the paper sack.

"I'll be very careful, thank you," Elizabeth said primly, flipping down the visor to study her reflection in the mirror. Reaching into her purse, she pulled out a brush, ran it through the long strands of her hair and applied fresh lip gloss.

Studying her, Michael thought again how she needed so little to make her naturally pretty, and he was grateful for the zillionth time that he had married her and somehow managed to hang on to her through the hardships.

"Ready?" he asked when she had finished and flipped the visor back in place.

"Ready." She smiled back at him.

They got out of the Blazer, and Michael deposited their sack in the garbage container. Then they walked toward the point where they imagined Wyn and Mary had stood.

"Okay, I have to go to the little boys room over there," Michael said.

"And I'm going to wander to that first lookout while I wait for you," she said, wondering if that's how the conversation had gone.

Michael turned and headed for the wooden structure that provided relief facilities, and she turned to study the trail. It seemed obvious to her that if Mary were going to look at the view, she would take the left trail, where she spotted a lookout. This was just as Wyn had described, so she headed in that direction.

The view was incredible from this vantage point. Placing her hands on her hips, she looked right to left, then turned and looked back over her shoulder.

"Michael?" she called out. He didn't answer. Could he hear

her or was he just not acknowledging it? Slowly she edged her way to the drop-off. Most places had a guardrail, but this one did not.

Elizabeth felt a weakness penetrating her knees as she peered straight down into the vista far below. It was hard to see where she might have landed if her foot had slipped and she had gone over the ledge. She heard the crunch of footsteps and whirled, aware that her nerves were suddenly on edge. Michael was taking long steps down the trail, his head tilted curiously at her.

"What's wrong, Elizabeth? You look frightened."

"Take a look down there, and see what it does to the back of your knees," she warned, pointing at the drop-off.

Michael winced. "I see what you mean."

"Michael, I called out to you. Did you hear me from inside the building?" she asked.

He shook his head. "No, you're at least a quarter mile from the building, and the lumber appeared to be pretty thick."

"Okay, so that would explain why Wyn didn't hear Mary if she called out to him," Elizabeth reasoned, holding on to Michael as she peered at the valley again.

"How loud did you yell?"

"Loud enough that you should have heard me. It's pretty quiet here."

Michael nodded. "But Wyn and Mary were here on a Saturday. Maybe there were other voices. And remember, the van supposedly drove off about that time. The sound of an older vehicle might have drowned out her voice if she had called."

Elizabeth nodded. "And the old van could have had one of those loud mufflers."

Michael shook his head. "I just find it hard to believe that someone didn't see or hear her."

Elizabeth nodded. "Right, but, Michael, take another look down there. It's frightening."

Michael peered over the edge and caught his breath. "Looks like you fall to forever."

Elizabeth nodded solemnly as they thought about the situation. "I think Mary fell and landed somewhere down there and was never discovered," Elizabeth concluded.

Michael nodded and put a protective arm around Elizabeth's waist. "You may be right." He turned and looked east and west, then sighed. "About half a mile back up the highway I noticed a narrow road leading off the mountainside. It's probably used by forest rangers. I'd like to get down into that valley and have a look around. What do you say?"

"Good idea." Elizabeth's brown eyes were glowing. She loved being a part of his investigation. "I enjoy tagging along with you." She slipped her hand in his as they walked back to the Blazer. "In fact, I like watching you figure things out. You're quite a guy." She winked at him.

Michael winked back. "And you're a very good sport. Or at least I hope you can be, once we try that steep trail."

They returned to the Blazer, and Michael started the engine while Elizabeth stared at the setting. "If only trees could talk," she said on a sigh as Michael drove toward the turnoff. Once Michael guided the Blazer down the narrow trail, however, Elizabeth found herself scooting closer and closer to his side. The trail continued to narrow, and the road was so rutted in places that Michael had to stop and get out and study the road from all angles before they continued on. Once, he had to get out and haul a thick pine limb from the center of the trail before they could go further.

"Michael...." Elizabeth caught her breath as she peered

down the steep incline unprotected by guardrails. "I don't know about you, but I'd rather travel this on foot from here on."

Michael was peering over the steering wheel, his hands gripping the wheel tightly. "Don't worry; we're safe," he said.

"Your tone of voice isn't convincing. Sorry, Michael, but I'm not such a good sport after all. I really wish you'd turn around."

He braked gently and stopped the car. "Where do you suggest we turn around?"

Elizabeth's eyes widened at that question. She whirled and peered out the window on the passenger's side, then over the dash. "Oh no," she said, feeling sick. There was no turnaround anywhere. In fact, to try to back the car up would lead them straight off the mountainside. She gulped. "What are we going to do?"

"We'll follow your suggestion. I'll leave the car, and we'll hike for a while. We may decide this is ridiculous and leave the Blazer and walk out."

"Seriously, how will we get our vehicle back up that mountain?" she asked worriedly.

"Don't suppose you're up to pushing the car backwards."

"Get serious!" she snapped. "This is not one bit funny, and you know it. In fact, I think you're being very cruel, considering the fact that I'm a greenhorn at this detective work."

"Sorry, darling." He put his arm around her shoulder. "I didn't realize what I was putting us through when I made the turnoff. The reason I want to hike further down is to see if there is a wider place in the road to turn the Blazer around."

She nodded. "Maybe we'd better start praying. In fact, why didn't we think of that sooner?"

"Don't worry." He pressed his lips into the softness of her hair and kissed the top of her head. "Our guardian angel is with us."

She smiled up at him. "I'm counting on that."

They fell into step side by side, their hands clasped, as the cool pine scent drifted over them and the huge evergreens seemed to enfold them in their own special canopy of green.

"It is lovely," Elizabeth acknowledged, trying to be more positive about their plight.

"Yep. And quiet. Very quiet."

Only the sound of their footsteps on fallen leaves and an occasional broken twig echoed back to them. They were surrounded by utter silence. Half a mile down, the trail widened, providing a tight squeeze for the Blazer to make a turnaround, but it would work if Michael was very careful.

"I'll get out and direct you," Elizabeth said as their eyes shot to the wide area then back to each other.

"And I'll let you," Michael agreed as they stopped walking to catch their breath.

"How far do you think we've come?" she asked, peering at the road that led straight down into the valley.

"At least a mile. And I haven't seen anything along the way to indicate that another human being has traveled this path in months. I noticed tire marks up at the top of the road, but I'm sure someone smarter than us was turning around. Not even a government vehicle has been through here. Still, we had to check it out."

"I guess so," she said, frowning doubtfully.

He shaded his eyes as they walked out of the green canopy into a patch of sunlight. "Know what we could do?" he asked, his eyes glinting mysteriously.

"No, what?" she asked guardedly.

"We could rent some twelve-speed bikes and go all the way down."

"That might be a good idea if we had the leg muscles to

pump our way back up this long trail," she said, looking around. "Going down isn't the trick; coming back up is. Or are you trying to get rid of me?" she asked, lifting an eyebrow.

"You know I'm not trying to get rid of you. I never want to be away from you again. I'm just concerned that you could endure a tough ride like that."

"Now you know better than to toss out such a challenge. Yes, Michael Calloway," she argued stubbornly, "I'm up to it if we can stop for rest breaks every twenty minutes."

Michael shook his head, pretending to be serious. "That'll only slow me down. Why don't you stay at the chalet and—"

"I'll do no such thing! I'm coming with you just in case you barrel off the edge of this trail into the deep blue. If that should happen, I need to be along so I can go for help before we have another missing person to report."

"In that case, I think we'll have to continue our little adventure tomorrow." Michael grinned, taking her hand as they hiked back to the car. Both were out of breath, Elizabeth more than Michael, although she did her best to conceal the fact. Michael had noticed, however, and it only made him appreciate her more. He loved her determination and grit, her willingness to follow along on his assignments and try to be as tough as he was.

He put his arm around her and pressed a kiss to her forehead. "I meant it when I said you were a great sport."

"As a matter of fact, I agree," she replied flippantly. "Who else would go chasing down a mountainside after you?"

They laughed as they turned the last corner and spotted the Blazer. Michael glanced at his watch. "Do you realize we've agreed to be at the Wentworth house by six o'clock? That leaves us three hours to return, shower, call Katie, and drive over there."

"We could save time by using the Jacuzzi together." Elizabeth grinned up at him.

"What an excellent idea!" He grinned back, and their steps quickened.

THREE

A t exactly ten minutes before six, Michael and Elizabeth turned a curve and spotted the sprawling log home, all lit up, at the crest of a hill. They both stared, imagining the relaxing lifestyle the Wentworths must lead.

Although darkness spread like a velvet blanket around them, the night lights at each corner of the house accented its design and structure. The house was perfectly centered against the backdrop of the mountains. Elizabeth smiled as she took in the home and its lovely setting. "What a wonderful place to live," she said on a sigh.

"It is," Michael agreed, turning in beside a miniature log house that served as a mailbox. "And I have a feeling the interior will be even more impressive."

They drove up to the house, where large windows spilled pools of light across the wide front porch. Matching rocking chairs of natural oak graced the porch, and lush ferns hung from the rafters.

"Well, darling, this isn't Oak Shadows, but it's quite a place," Michael said, as he pulled to a stop and cut the engine.

"It's a wonderful place," Elizabeth said, studying the unique home.

"Shall we get out and go inside before they start to wonder about us?"

Elizabeth laughed and nodded. "I'm sure they're accustomed to people gawking at their house."

"It's very pretty," Michael agreed as he got out of the car and came around to open the door for Elizabeth. In the process, he couldn't help wondering if their life might not be better in this kind of rural mountain setting, which seemed to reflect tranquillity. But their work was in Atlanta, and he was now as proud of their home at Oak Shadows as Elizabeth had always been.

Clutching the small bouquet of flowers they had brought, Elizabeth followed Michael up the porch steps and knocked on the massive front door.

Matt opened the door with a friendly smile. "Michael, good to see you again." He extended his hand. "And you're Elizabeth, of course."

A tall man dressed in a navy V-neck sweater and jeans looked down at her. He was almost as tall as Michael, which made him over six feet, with long legs and broad shoulders. Thick, dark hair, cut short, framed a square face with nice features, deep blue eyes, and a friendly smile.

"It's nice to see you again, Matt," Michael said as they shook hands.

"Please come in, but be sure to watch your step. Although we try to pick up after Trey, we sometimes miss something here and there."

"Oh, we understand. We're parents too," Elizabeth laughed, linking her hand in Michael's as they followed Matt inside.

Matt led them into the great room. It was a huge room, at least thirty by twenty-eight feet, with lots of glass and a stone fireplace in the end wall. The room was done in shades of green splashed with pale gold, and with the soft interior lighting, Elizabeth had the sensation of standing in an enchanted forest bathed in sunlight.

"How lovely," she exclaimed.

"Thanks. Laurel will be right with us. She wanted to change

out of her jeans, but I stayed comfortable." He indicated his own. "One of my resolutions for living here was giving up the suit and tie, and it's transformed me into something of a slob, I'm afraid."

"You look very comfortable, and I can't help envying you," Michael said, relieved that he had worn casual slacks and a sweater. "This is really an interesting room," he added, thrusting his hands in his pockets and looking around.

"All our furniture is handmade, from the arts-and-crafts center," Matt informed them as his eyes followed theirs across the room. "We have so much talent in this area that it seemed a crime not to utilize it in our own home."

"You're right," Elizabeth replied, looking from intricately carved tables and chairs to the matching sofas done in green and gold. Afghans in complimentary colors lay casually over sofa backs. Huge gold pillows were placed on the hardwood floor just past a hand-loomed rug, near the fireplace. A smaller pillow lay between the two. Elizabeth figured this was where their little family of three gathered on cold evenings. The walls were filled with lovely oil paintings, a few watercolors, and some interesting black-and-white sketches spaced about. She recognized the artist's name on the paintings. She had seen the same ones in the shop.

"Hi," Laurel called from the doorway. She was holding a small boy who was a tiny replica of his father except for the big brown eyes, which were a gift from his mother.

"Hi, there," Elizabeth called, walking over to their side.

"This is James Matthew Wentworth III, but we call him Trey," Laurel announced, her voice rich with pride. She tilted her head to look down at her son. "Can you say hi to our guests, Trey?"

"Hi!" Trey repeated, showing off his dimples as he smiled.

"You are a very handsome one," Elizabeth said, reaching out to touch the chubby little fist that clutched a green rubber ball. He was wearing red overalls and a long-sleeved navy T-shirt that complimented his thick dark hair. "He just turned two," Laurel explained, "and he stays quite busy. Consequently, so do I. My grandmother absolutely dotes on him and comes over to keep him while I work at the shop."

"That's a nice arrangement," Elizabeth said, wishing with all of her heart that her beloved grandmother were still alive. "When is your other one due?" She inquired.

"The doctor says March; I say February."

"Then it will probably be February." Elizabeth smiled at her, and they exchanged the knowing gaze of two mothers who share similar experiences.

"Right!" Laurel shook her head. Her hair was swept back in a ponytail, and she wore little makeup, but Elizabeth could see that for this woman makeup would be a waste. She had smooth skin, nice features, and large eyes that alternately danced with glee or reflected a heart filled with love as she looked from her son to her husband.

The men had already fallen into conversation over a World War I book Michael had spotted in the built-in bookshelf.

"Michael is also a history buff," Elizabeth said, turning back to admire Trey again.

"I bought the book for Matt last year. I like history too. In fact, I taught school before I married Matt."

"Oh? I didn't know that. Did you enjoy teaching?"

Laurel nodded. "I loved it. But now I just want to be a mommy for a while." Laurel smiled at Elizabeth. "Want to come into the kitchen and chat with me while I feed Trey?"

"Sure."

Trey was reaching toward something in Elizabeth's hand,

and she suddenly remembered the flowers. "Oh, these are for you." She handed Laurel the small bouquet of autumn flowers they had purchased from a vendor on their way through Angel Valley.

"How thoughtful of you," Laurel said, shifting Trey in her arms to take the bouquet. "On second thought, maybe I'll put you down," she said, planting him solidly on the floor. "Just don't get into mischief," she warned lovingly, then looked at Elizabeth. "I adore flowers and try to keep something in the house throughout the year to give us a feeling of nature when there's snow three feet deep."

"I noticed how healthy your ferns are."

Laurel nodded. "I'll soon be bringing them in for the winter. Our current project is carving the ten-pound pumpkin that Matt brought in from Pigeon Forge. It will take some real artwork to do it justice. Angel Valley goes all out for decorating the seasons of the year, as you may have noticed. In September we start with pumpkins; then we switch to cartoon characters for Halloween; then the first week in November the Christmas lights go up."

"Sounds like a lot of fun," Elizabeth said, following her into a huge kitchen.

"Yes, it is a lot of fun. I suppose that's why I never want to live anywhere else." She glanced back over her shoulder at Elizabeth. "Actually, I lived in Marietta for a year when I was teaching."

"Marietta? Really? That's our area."

She nodded. "So Matt told me. I just couldn't adjust to the busyness there after growing up here. But then you and Michael would probably be bored to death if you moved from the city here."

"I don't know," Elizabeth sighed. "I think it would take me a long time to tire of the tranquillity that just seems to rub off, not to mention the beauty and the friendliness of the people all around."

"Incidentally, I hope you'll get to meet my grandmother while you're here. She's very special to me."

"Oh really? My grandmother was special to me too. I was actually closer to her than to my mother."

"Is that right?" Laurel looked at her with interest as she opened a drawer and removed a gloved pot holder. "My father was killed in service and—"

"So was mine," Elizabeth said, as both women stared at each other. "We seem to have a lot in common!"

"Isn't that interesting?" Laurel smiled. "And I was wondering this afternoon what subjects we would discuss. Since you're a psychologist, I hadn't guessed there would be so many things to talk about because I confess to knowing little about psychology."

"But you know a lot about life. And I saw your family Bible in the living room. Would you believe that Michael and I have a large family Bible exactly like that one?"

"Really?" Laurel laughed. "That's amazing. But I can tell you for sure that God's Word has been a very important part of our life and our marriage."

"Ours too," Elizabeth admitted, taking a seat in the kitchen chair and then standing up again. "Oh, tell me what I can do to help. I don't want to be treated like company."

"Okay, I'll put you to work in a minute, although I must confess that most everything is already done. I prepared a chicken casserole and tossed a salad. Oh, and I have apple dumplings from a special shop here that I adore."

"Sounds wonderful," Elizabeth replied, glancing back at Trey, whose chubby little hands had latched onto another rubber ball. Looking at him with tenderness, Elizabeth was aware that she had begun to feel a longing for another baby. There had been so many other things to occupy their minds that another child had not seemed possible. But again the old familiar ache was nudging her. "Could you show me your green ball, Trey?" Elizabeth asked kindly.

In response he bounced the ball in her direction.

"Careful, Trey," Laurel laughed. "We don't need a ball as the centerpiece for our casserole."

Both women laughed. "Just tell me when you want me to do something," Elizabeth offered, watching Laurel place the large casserole dish in the center of the dining-room table and then hurry back for a crystal bowl of garden salad.

"If you entertain Trey, as you are doing now, that's an enormous help." She glanced back at Elizabeth. "You mentioned a little girl. Tell me about her."

Elizabeth was filled with tenderness at the mention of her daughter. "Katie will soon be nine. Needless to say, she's a bit spoiled, but we adore her."

Laurel nodded. "That's understandable. Tell me about yourself. You must lead a very interesting life."

She sighed. "It's been a bit too interesting lately," she said, reaching out to catch the offhand ball tossed at her. She rolled it back to him.

"Oh?" Laurel cocked an eyebrow. "Now that kind of statement really sparks my curiosity."

"Well," Elizabeth sighed, "there's a lot I could tell. Maybe if we have more private time together, I can do that. The latest incident was a bout of amnesia after being struck by a car in a hit-and-run incident."

Laurel stopped in the center of the kitchen, salad bowls in hand. "How terrible for you. I read something about it in the papers, but the story didn't go into detail. What happened?"

Elizabeth tried to give her the short version of the story, finishing with the return of her memory and the capture of Dr. Phillips.

Laurel moved quietly around the kitchen, finishing up the meal while listening intently to everything Elizabeth had told her. Then the smell of burning bread jolted them back to reality.

"Oh no!" Laurel exclaimed, turning toward the oven.

At that point, Matt had entered the kitchen, following the scent, but he merely laughed as she pulled out the garlic toast, totally black. "Darling, when you're pregnant, you're allowed to burn everything but the house and our guests." Matt grinned at her.

"I really don't think I should burn you and Trey, either," she teased back.

Suddenly they were all laughing; even Michael had joined in from the doorway.

"We don't need bread," Elizabeth said, looking from Laurel to Matt.

"Believe me," Michael said, grinning, "from what I see on the dining-room table, there's more than enough food. Please don't worry about the bread."

Elizabeth smiled at Michael, appreciating his consideration. He was the same way with her, and she realized how blessed she had been. She could see that Laurel and Matt were close as well.

Everyone pitched in to finish up the meal preparations, and soon they were seated in the dining room. Matt and Laurel sat at opposite ends of the table; Elizabeth and Michael sat together on one side while the other side was reserved for Trey, who seemed to require plenty of space. Laurel had placed a large sheet of plastic under his chair to allow for spills.

Laurel grasped Matt's hand, and automatically Elizabeth and Michael did the same, as all bowed their heads, and Matt gave thanks for the food.

Afterward, they dug heartily into the meal, which was excellent. For several minutes only the clang of silver on china and an occasional "Pass me" broke the companionable silence.

Finally Michael spoke up. "Laurel, you're a wonderful cook."

"Well, thank you. Everything I know I learned from Granny. By the way, you must meet her while you're here!" Laurel's brown eyes sparkled. "She lives out on the edge of Angel Valley in the same house she's had since the day she married, and the land has been in our family for generations. It would be a real treat for Granny to meet someone as sophisticated as you two!"

Elizabeth laughed. "We don't think of ourselves as sophisticated."

"Personally, I would love to hear about some of your cases, Michael," Matt said.

"Your brother Jay made quite a splash in the papers when he solved that mysterious kidnapping during the '96 Olympics. And then Laurel and I were both fascinated to read about what happened to you, Elizabeth. You may not want to talk about it."

"She already has," Laurel piped up, proud of her knowledge. "She told me all about it in the kitchen just now."

"Both cases were linked in an odd way," Michael explained. "The psychiatrist who married Julie, the woman who came to me to find her missing twin—"

"Oh, yes, I want to hear about that—"

"Darling, let him finish one case before we pump him about the other one."

"Well," Laurel rolled her eyes, "you know my thirst for

adventure. Life is pretty limited up here in Angel Valley, but then after hearing about these cases, I think I'm glad that we lead such a quiet life."

First Michael, then Elizabeth, began reciting the bizarre things that had happened to them in the past. By the time both had finished, Matt and Laurel sat with their mouths wide open, oblivious to the fact that Trey wanted down out of the high chair.

Enjoying the task, Elizabeth reached over to wipe his mouth, then glanced questioningly at his mother. "He's eaten everything on his plate."

Laurel's stunned eyes wandered back to her son. "Oh. Trey, drink all your milk and then you're through."

She got up out of her seat and ambled around the table. Watching her, Elizabeth recalled how she had felt during her pregnancy—a bit awkward, even clumsy at times, yet always filled with a sense of delight over the little being within her.

"Here, I'll take him," Matt offered, coming around to pull Trey out of his high chair.

"Thanks, hon." Laurel turned back to them. "Let's have coffee and let our meal settle," she suggested, glancing at Elizabeth.

"The dishes—"

"Later!" Laurel was emphatic. "I'm serious. I really would prefer to sit in there, away from the leftovers, and continue our conversation."

"Then I'll help you later," Elizabeth insisted.

The group moved back to the great room, where Matt positioned Trey in his lap in the recliner, Laurel took a seat in a matching recliner, and Elizabeth and Michael settled onto the comfortable sofa.

"Matt, you've done a great job with the improvements in Angel Valley," Michael began.

Laurel smiled proudly. "He has, hasn't he? And he has remained on the board of his family's real estate corporation in Atlanta."

"I still have to be in Atlanta once a week," he explained, "and I troubleshoot for our Knoxville office. Fortunately I'm able to do much of this work through fax and e-mail. The business here is my main interest. As for its success—" he looked at Laurel— "don't leave yourself out." He looked back at Michael and Elizabeth. "All I did was point this community in the right direction. The talent here is incredible."

"I could see that," Elizabeth replied. "It's amazing to find so much talent clustered in one area."

"You have to understand the mountain people," Laurel began slowly, her eyes drifting upward as though thinking of each one. "Many of them have learned their trade from their parents or grandparents. They're homebodies and love creating things. But they're very resistant to change. For example " she exchanged an amused glance with Matt—"Wilbur Tinsley refused to change his service station. He said it had been good enough for his father and grandfather, and it would be good enough for him to pass on to his son."

"You have to respect their opinions and attitudes, and we've tried to do that," Matt explained. "The only way I would even attempt to market their wares is through our store and a mail-order catalog. The catalog features items from the shop. I have it printed up and mailed out from Atlanta. We get orders from all over the United States. This cuts down on incoming traffic while supplying a healthy income for those whose work is ordered."

"How do you distribute the items?" Elizabeth asked.

"We have trucks on the road, delivering goods."

"And there are always reorders on items," Laurel said.

"Sounds like a wonderful marketing technique," Michael acknowledged. "Since you're so good at sizing up a situation, maybe I should ask your advice on locating Mary Chamblis."

Matt took a deep breath. "I'd be out of my turf on that one, I'm afraid."

"Elizabeth and I drove up to Painted Rock today and looked around. We even took one of the forest service roads down into that valley."

"Wow, you're brave!" Laurel exclaimed.

"Maybe we're just foolish," Elizabeth said, half smiling as she glanced at Michael. "I have to admit that at one point I was feeling a bit shaky. But then Michael found a turnaround, and we made it out of there."

"I know the search-and-rescue team put in a lot of time on this, but don't you think it's possible her body could have been overlooked?" Michael asked frankly, directing the question to Matt.

Matt nodded. "I think that's what happened. This is a vast area, and there are hundreds of hiking trails throughout the Smokies, but the search-and-rescue teams are pretty thorough. They know all the hills and hollows. It's hard to figure it out," he said, reaching down to hand Trey another toy.

"I just had an idea," Laurel said. "There's a guy here from UT who has taken a year off from his graduate studies to do research on the mountain people. His name is Ben Thornton, and he's spent weeks traveling the back roads, getting to know folks back in the coves who aren't always congenial to outsiders. Why don't you talk to Ben? Maybe he'd accompany you on a trip around the back country, or at least he might give you some information that would be helpful."

"Great suggestion," Michael said, removing the notebook and pen from his pocket.

"Ben Thornton, you said. And where would I find him?"

Laurel looked at Matt. "Good question. Do you know where Ben is this week?"

He shook his head. "Last I heard, he was over in Cherokee, but you could check with Millie at the post office. He gets his mail here general delivery."

"I should have thought of Millie," Laurel laughed. "She keeps tabs on everybody in the valley and on any stranger who comes to town. If you haven't met her, get ready. She's a bit nosy, but she has a heart of gold."

Michael was still making notes.

"Mommy, wanna go to bed." Trey had left his toys and gone to his mother's chair, tugging on her skirt.

She reached out and gave him a hug. "It is getting to be that time for you, isn't it, sweetie?"

Elizabeth looked at Michael. "We should be going too. But Laurel, I want to help you with the dishes."

"Nope," Matt said, coming to his feet. "That's my job. Whoever doesn't cook gets kitchen duty afterwards. Especially now, with Laurel tiring easily."

Michael stood, extending his hand to Elizabeth to pull her up. "If we can't help, then we're going to say good night. Laurel, the dinner was wonderful. We'd like to take you guys out whenever you're free."

"Thanks." Laurel smiled, lifting Trey. "We thoroughly enjoyed having you. Trey, can you say good night to our friends, please?"

"'Night," he said, the brown eyes drooping.

"Good night, Trey." Elizabeth walked over to pat his little shoulder. "Laurel, thanks for everything. I'll be in the shop to see you soon."

After they had said their good nights and departed, Elizabeth was thoughtful as Michael drove them back to the chalet.

"What's in that pretty head of yours?" Michael asked.

She rolled her head on the seat and directed her gaze toward Michael. "You know, I think I'm ready for another child. What about you?"

Michael's eyebrows arched. "Really?" He turned back to the highway, staring thoughtfully into the darkness. "Trey is a cute little fellow, isn't he?"

"We might get another girl," Elizabeth reminded him.

Michael grinned across at her. "I wouldn't mind."

He reached for her hand, and they rode along in silence, each feeling a deep sense of contentment.

The next morning Michael left Elizabeth sleeping and drove into Angel Valley. His first stop was the post office. Glancing at his watch, he noticed it was only two minutes past eight, but a few people were already shuffling in to get their mail. Michael waited his turn to speak with the postmistress, who was every bit as inquisitive as Laurel had warned, once he introduced himself and gave her a business card.

Millie was a thin, gray-haired woman whose small bifocals perched precariously on the end of her nose. Her dark eyes appraised Michael quickly as she pocketed his business card in her skirt. She wore a navy pleated skirt and a red cardigan reminiscent of the fifties, but Michael had a feeling she wouldn't care what he thought about her idea of fashion.

"Ben usually checks his mail once or twice a week," Millie informed him. "Since he hasn't been in all week, I'd say he'll be here this morning. He knows I close at noon on Saturday, so if I'm not badly mistaken, I'll be seeing him soon. What do you want me to tell him?"

"We're staying at Windwhispers," he began, although she was already nodding her head as though she knew. He tried to suppress a grin as he remembered what Laurel had told him about Millie's inquisitive nature. "The phone number is—"

"I have it," she cut in, smiling. "Are you going back there now?"

"As a matter of fact, I am. So will you please have him call me?"

"Think he can help you find Mary Chamblis?" Having studied his business card, she got right to the point.

"I hope so. I understand he knows the area well, and that's why I wanted to talk to him." He decided to test Millie's knowledge. "Don't suppose you have any theories on this case, do you?"

She shrugged, her lips pressed together in a hard line. "Maybe."

"Well, would you mind sharing your opinion?" he asked, giving her his best smile. "Her fiancé is really worried."

"Is he?" she cocked an eyebrow.

He leaned closer, like a hunter circling his prey. "Well, he certainly seemed concerned, but looks can be deceiving, don't you think?" He watched her carefully, wondering exactly what she knew that he didn't.

"Yep. These rich folks drift in here, make a mess of things, then expect us to solve their problems. But I don't mean to disparage everyone. Matt Wentworth is rich, but he is a nice man who decided to invest his money here."

"Oh? I thought maybe Laurel had something to do with it."

Millie grinned at him, enjoying the game. "She did. But his uppity mother and sister thought we were all just a bunch of idiots until their plane went down in the mountains and the volunteer search-and-rescue folks found the plane and saved their lives."

Michael shook his head. "Wow. That's amazing. So do you know something about Mary Chamblis that might help? Has there been something in the mail?"

"Nothing on Mary Chamblis. But I didn't like the way that rich fella—what's his name?"

"Wyn Dalton."

"Dalton." She nodded. "He was going around town demanding to know if anybody had seen her. That's not the way you approach people here. We're glad to pitch in and help, but we don't like being told what to do by outsiders."

"I understand," Michael said slowly, making a mental note of those words. "Well, as you can see, I'm asking for help. It isn't my nature to make demands on people, and I sincerely appreciate all the help I can get. After all, there's a young woman lost somewhere down in that valley—"

"Maybe she isn't lost."

Michael frowned. "May I ask exactly what you mean by that remark, Millie?"

She shrugged. "Looks like to me, she would have been found if she was lost. Unless she took a fall, got up half addled, and wandered off into a cove somewhere. Then somebody would have found her and brought her in." She frowned and pursed her lips. "Come to think of it, there are two or three families back up in those hills who wouldn't bring her in. Fact is, they wouldn't want her to leave."

Michael's heart was beating faster. His instincts told him that for the first time he was onto something concrete.

"Millie, if you were to mention the names of those families, I would forget just exactly where the information came from, but it would certainly give me a starting point. She really is a nice girl," he said in a soft, pleading voice, "and she can't help it if Wyn Dalton was rude."

She nodded. "You're right about that. The Stringfellows up at Cold Creek, the Dawsons over on Blackberry Ridge, and the Birdsongs, maybe. Although I think Jasper and the sheriff questioned all of them. But if you decide to go back in there, you better not go without a weapon."

Michael's eyes widened. "They're that bad, huh?"

She nodded. "They believe in protecting their territory."

"Did Ben Thornton make friends with them?"

She shook her head. "I doubt it. You don't make friends with the Stringfellows or the Dawsons unless you're one of them."

He nodded. "Want to tell me how to get there?"

"Ben can tell you. He knows the way, but I doubt that he ever got within a quarter mile of their porch before Buster cut down on him."

"Buster?"

"The Stringfellow boy. He rides shotgun on the place most of the time."

Michael shook his head. "Then I better go in with a posse, don't you think?"

Millie laughed. "You couldn't gather a posse around Angel Valley to go up against the Dawsons, or especially the Stringfellows."

"Then what would you suggest?" He eyed her with a mixture of frustration and amusement.

"Give a holler that you want to buy something. That might get you past the first bend in the road." She laughed and shook her head. "I'm just teasing you, son. But the truth is, they're pretty rough. If Mary Chamblis ended up on their property, I doubt if she left."

Michael stared at her. "How far do they live from Painted Rock?"

"The Dawson place is a couple of miles up that back ridge, but the Stringfellows—" she paused, chewing her lip—"there's a shortcut, and Ben might have found it; he's always studying those maps of his. I haven't been up in there in twenty years, but there used to be an old trail that cut through from the base of Painted Rock over to the Stringfellow property line."

"And you don't think the sheriff has checked that out?"

"He probably did. But why would the Stringfellows start being truthful now? For them it's just as easy to spin a tale however they want to, and that is exactly their habit."

"So their property wasn't searched?"

"Wouldn't be any reason to search their property. Nobody has any proof that your Mary Chamblis would be there. And if they said she wasn't there, then what would you do?"

"Good question. But you think that's the most likely explanation of what's happened to her?"

She hesitated as the front door opened and an elderly gentleman wearing a baseball cap, jeans, and denim jacket ambled in.

"Clarence, I've been wondering when you'd get back from visiting your son."

Michael hesitated for only a moment after realizing that Millie was not going to introduce him. Oh well, he supposed she had her reasons.

"Good day," he said, smiling at her.

"Good day," she said, her reserve back in place again.

"Sounds as though this Millie just has a vivid imagination, Michael," Elizabeth protested, as Michael related the news to her while they sat on the deck of their chalet, enjoying the bright sunshine while munching the fresh sweet rolls from the bakery.

Elizabeth paused, taking a sip of coffee. "In this day and time, people just don't live like that anymore. Come on, Michael; I think Millie, the inquisitive postmistress, is pulling your leg."

"She may be," Michael said, reaching for another cinnamon roll. "But I can't ignore the first lead I've had."

"And you consider this lady, whom Laurel hints is a gossiper, to be a reliable lead? I can't believe you'd put that much stock in what she said, Michael." She finished her sweet roll, licked her lips as though enjoying the last taste, then touched a napkin to her mouth.

Michael shrugged. "You could be right. But I have a feeling there may be some truth to what she told me. Maybe I'm crazy, but I think I should at least investigate the possibility of Mary's being held captive by the Stringfellows."

"Then investigate with the sheriff by your side."

Michael chuckled. "It so happens that he's gone on a Boy Scout outing with his grandson, and Jasper is in charge again. I'd rather have you along for protection than Jasper." He winked at her. "You're a lot cuter, and I think you could talk us out of a tight situation much quicker than Jasper. In fact, I wouldn't even take him with me. Buster, as Millie calls him, would be sure to unload his Winchester if he spotted big bad Jasper!"

Elizabeth tilted her head to the side and studied him with curiosity. "So just what do you plan to do, Michael?"

He lifted his wrist and checked his watch. "Apparently Ben Thornton didn't get back into town to check his mail. It's after two, and the post office closed at noon. He hasn't called. Want to take a ride with me? And then a hike?"

She groaned. "Are we going to see the Stringfellows?"

Michael laughed. "No, in all seriousness, I wouldn't go there yet. What I do want to do is go back to Painted Rock and explore that west trail. It should be easy walking, so you needn't be dreading another heart-pounding hike along a steep trail."

"That's a relief," Elizabeth sighed.

Soon they were warmly dressed and back in the Blazer. This time they had made coffee and filled a thermos bottle to take with them, along with some apples and cheese. Also, Elizabeth had sneaked in a package of sugar wafers, knowing they were Michael's favorite treat.

They drove to Painted Rock, with each alternately speculating on what might have happened. Elizabeth's best theory was that Mary had fallen and not been discovered. Michael knew that was the general opinion, but something about that didn't sit right with him. He couldn't even say why. Still, he always paid attention to his instincts. He had a way of picking up on facts that his subconscious then slowly worked through to the finish.

Michael turned the Blazer into the parking area where two trucks and a car were also parked. He and Elizabeth began to scan the area around them. Today was Saturday, and there would be more people milling up and down the trail to Painted Rock. This seemed more typical of the day Mary disappeared, and that pleased Michael.

"Okay." He turned to Elizabeth. "Let's explore the theory that she went along the west trail to the lookout. We'll head there first."

They got out, locked the car, and looked around. There was an older couple slowly making their way up the main trail to the summit of Painted Rock. A boy and girl about seventeen were returning to a truck. Smiling into each other's faces, their arms linked together, the young couple didn't appear to have their minds on the scenery. Once Elizabeth and Michael reached the overlook, he pulled the binoculars from around his neck and scanned the valley below. Evergreens and colorful flora filled his vision; nothing else.

"Michael, I have an idea," Elizabeth said, planting her hands on her hips. "Let's just suppose that Mary spotted something further down the trail—maybe a doe darted out. So, instead of taking the assumed route, she wanders off in the direction that warns of bears and wild animals."

"Okay, that's a reasonable assumption."

They started down the trail. Michael had stopped to scan again with his binoculars and was not paying attention to the path. Elizabeth, concentrating on a beautiful oak tree overhead, didn't see the limb blocking her path. She tripped over it, plunging headlong down the trail, arms flailing. She wrapped her arms around the trunk of a pine to break her fall and ended up half sprawled beside the tree. She stared at her right leg, which was throbbing from her collision with the tree limb.

Michael was instantly at her side, kneeling down to put his arms around her. "Are you okay? Can you stand? Is anything broken?"

"Take it easy, Michael. I'm okay," she said as she rubbed her leg. "Just a bit clumsy, that's all." When he helped her up, however, she winced and noticed for the first time that there was a nasty scrape on her arm to go with the bruise forming on her leg.

"Okay, the hike is over," he said.

"This is silly," she tried to protest. "I can go on."

"But do you want to?" he asked, checking her arm.

"It just needs a Band-Aid," she said meekly. "But my leg is starting to ache. No, to be truthful, I'd rather go back and curl up on the sofa. Sorry, Michael. Guess I'm not too good at this detective business."

"Hey, don't say that. You've been a real trooper! Everyone takes a fall now and then. Why should you be any different?"

"Oh, Michael, I hate myself for being so clumsy."

"You weren't clumsy. There are all kinds of things around to trip up a lady."

Suddenly their eyes locked on each other and widened.

"Maybe that's it!" Elizabeth turned her head and looked back at the trail. "Maybe she fell and rolled further down that hill. Oh, Michael, you have to check it out. Follow that trail and see if—"

"No point in doing that." He shook his head. "She wouldn't have rolled for a mile. The sheriff and his men already followed the trail at least that far. I'm sure the search-and-rescue combed all of this area as well. Anyway, I don't even care about that now. Let's go back to the chalet."

"I'm so sorry," she said, shaking her head. "I so wanted to be a good companion on this little expedition."

"You *are* a good companion and an excellent sport about everything," he said tenderly, kissing her forehead. "Now let's give up the search for the rest of the day."

As soon as they were settled in the Blazer, Michael reached into the back seat for the thermos of coffee. He poured some of the steaming liquid into the thermos cup and shared it with Elizabeth as they sat quietly with only the engine running and the heater turned on full blast.

"I have something else," she said with a teasing smile. Reaching under her seat, she pulled out the package of sugar wafers and waved them at Michael.

He laughed and shook his head. "You're just full of surprises."

They shared the coffee and a handful of cookies as they sat quietly munching and staring out at the breathtaking view.

After a thoughtful pause Michael spoke up. "You know, sitting here looking out at the mist in the valleys makes me recall what Wyn said about Mary's comparing the fog to spirits. That strikes me as a rather odd thing to say, coming from someone who seemed quite practical by today's standards."

Elizabeth reached for another cookie and tilted her head up at Michael. "Maybe she doesn't know there is only one great Spirit. The holy one."

Michael nodded slowly, taking a sip of coffee. "I don't get the feeling that either she or Wyn are particularly religious, do you?"

"Well, I don't think we can make that kind of call just yet. I do get the feeling that he is not a faith-filled kind of guy. Or maybe it's just that he is focused only on finding his fiancée. Anyway, who are we to judge?"

"You're right, of course." Michael sighed. "I dread calling to inform him that we're getting nowhere at all on this case."

"Maybe you could delay that phone call. After all, you're doing the best you can with what you have to go on."

He shrugged. "Yeah, I guess. Well, let's get back to our cozy den," he said, finishing off his coffee. Elizabeth recapped the thermos and folded the package of sugar wafers, noting they had demolished at least half of them. Michael shifted gears and backed the Blazer out of its parking space. "So far, all the day has brought us is a fall for you and another question about Mary Chamblis for me."

When they turned into the driveway winding up to their chalet, they spotted a gray pickup truck parked out in the front.

"We have company," Elizabeth said with surprise, glancing across at Michael.

FOUR

A young man in his midtwenties with wavy blond hair and a pleasant face was walking down the steps of their chalet, heading back to the truck. He had obviously been up to knock on their door and, getting no response, was about to leave. He was wearing the kind of clothing outdoorsmen wore: good hiking boots, thick jeans, layered sweater with a plaid shirt collar peeking over the top of the sweater.

Michael wheeled in beside the truck and rolled down the window. "Hi, I'm Michael Calloway."

A friendly smile broke over the young man's face as he walked over to their parked vehicle, circling to the driver's side. "Hi, I'm Ben Thornton." He extended his hand to Michael. "Millie said you wanted to see me."

"I do, and I appreciate you making the drive up." Michael shook his hand, then got out of the Blazer and came around to open the door for Elizabeth although she was already getting out. "This is my wife, Elizabeth. Or maybe I should say my patient, Elizabeth. We were hiking up at Painted Rock, and she took a fall."

Ben was instantly concerned. "Oh? What—"

"I'm fine, really." She extended a hand to Ben. "Nothing's wrong that a Band-Aid and an ice pack won't fix."

Michael put his arm around Elizabeth, steadying her, then turned back to their guest.

"Ben, do you have any plans for the next couple of hours?" Michael asked.

"Not really." He shrugged. "I just got back in town at noon."

Michael glanced at Ben's truck and spotted a forestry map folded on the dash. "Why don't you grab your map and come in? We'll rustle up some sandwiches."

"Sounds good to me." Ben nodded, opening the door of his truck to retrieve the map.

"You probably heard from Millie that I'm here to investigate the disappearance of Mary Chamblis," Michael said as they entered the chalet.

"Yes, she told me. I don't know how I can help you. Several people have already asked if I've seen or heard anything about her on my travels, and the answer is no. Still, I'll be glad to come in and visit with you, give you the benefit of what I've learned about the area."

Soon Ben and Michael were seated at the kitchen table, the forestry map spread out before them. Elizabeth was nestled comfortably on the sofa, ready to doze off, in spite of her desire to listen to the conversation.

"This is as far as we went today," Michael explained, tracing their route with his forefinger on Ben's map. "But I'm curious about an old trail that shortcuts over this mountain." He tapped a stretch of property.

Ben studied the map, nodding. "I know the area, but I've never been over that particular trail." His brow furrowed beneath his blond hair. "From Painted Rock, the trail circles back onto the main trail. That west trail twists and turns back until you're actually traveling east. It would be easy for some-one to get lost there. This mountain range straddles the Tennessee-North Carolina border. If you continue on, you've crossed the North Carolina border, and you're not far from the Cherokee reservation and the small town of Cherokee."

Michael nodded, pointing at the origins of the west trail.

"Due to the remoteness, that trail would be the most logical one to take if someone were abducting her. Right?"

Ben considered the question. "Yes, I guess so."

"Tell me something." Michael studied the map again. "Millie mentioned an old trail that would shortcut over to the Stringfellow property."

Ben winced. "You don't want to go there," he said, visibly tensing. "Not without the sheriff and some of his people. They're the only folks who wouldn't let me on their property. I even got to talk to the Dawsons for a minute, just a minute, mind you. But they didn't threaten to blow my head off. The Stringfellows did." Ben studied the map again. "There's a steep rugged trail crossing the mountain, but you're right. It looks like it's possible to take a shortcut over that mountain and come out on the other side near the Stringfellow place."

Michael was thoughtful for a moment; then he leaned back in his chair and looked at Ben. "I'm beginning to suspect that's where she is."

Ben's eyes widened. "You really think so? But why wouldn't they try to get ransom money? It's pretty well known that Dalton is rich and could pay."

He shrugged. "There has to be another reason. Tell me what you know about the family."

Ben leaned back in the chair, thinking. "There's a woman with a face like a hawk's, and at least three wild-looking guys. I guess the sons are in their late twenties and early thirties. The oldest one must be midthirties."

"Which one is Buster?" Michael asked with a grin.

Ben's eyebrow hiked. "He's the oldest. He's also the one who told me to get off their property. I tried to explain that I didn't want to bother them, but he wasn't listening. He just leveled his Winchester at me."

"Why are they so protective of their property?"

"The Dawsons say they're just mean, that it's born and bred into them. The old man claims to have shot three men for trespassing." Ben hesitated. "I have no proof of it, but when I was hiking up some back roads, I saw a strange-looking patch out back of their house. I'm guessing it's marijuana. But I could be wrong."

Michael nodded. "Makes sense. Still, I have to talk with them. I wouldn't be a good detective if I didn't follow every lead. And right now, the people back up in those hidden coves seem to be the most likely suspects in Mary's disappearance."

Ben laced his fingers around his blond head and stared at Michael. "I just don't see why they would want to hide a woman there. That's the point—they don't like outsiders."

"Are the guys married?"

He shrugged. "I don't think so. In fact, I'm sure Millie said they were bachelors."

"Then maybe that's your answer."

But even as he mentioned that possibility, Michael himself wasn't convinced. From what he knew of the really clannish types, they would go out of their way to avoid someone like Mary. But sometimes there was no figuring out motives; people often reacted instinctively and paid the consequences later.

"Ben, if you don't have plans, I'd like to hire you to be my guide tomorrow. Are you free?"

"It's the only day I *am* free. I have an appointment every day next week."

Michael glanced back at Elizabeth. "Do you mind being alone for a few hours, hon?"

"No. But I guess this means we won't be attending that lovely little chapel down the road. Tomorrow *is* Sunday."

Ben frowned. "I wish I had another free day."

Michael looked from Ben to Elizabeth. "I'm afraid we have no choice. Maybe we can attend church later." He turned back to Ben. "So you want to go to the Stringfellows' tomorrow?"

"You've aroused my curiosity. I'd like a chance at learning more about those people. They must have some amazing stories to tell." Ben thought for a moment, then grinned. "If you can make friends with the Stringfellows, I definitely want to be along."

"Then why don't you come over in the morning?" Michael suggested.

"Sure. How early do you want to start?"

Michael scratched his head. "Is seven too early?"

"Nope, I'm an early riser." Ben stood, folding his map back into a neat square.

"Great." Michael pushed back his chair and followed Ben to the door. Glancing out, he had another thought. "Do you mind if we take your truck? It might be better at navigating any narrow roads."

"Fine. We can drive around, and then if you want, we can park the truck and hike in from there to the Stringfellow property." He pressed a hand to the back of his neck. "I guess I'm willing to give that another try."

"Don't worry," Michael laughed. "We won't get too adventurous."

Ben nodded at that and then looked across at Elizabeth. "I certainly hope those sore spots heal in a hurry. Junior Foster, back up at Yellow Creek Cove, would probably tell you to apply some bee venom to the bruises."

"Bee venom?" Elizabeth echoed, looking as though she had not heard correctly.

Ben chuckled. "That's right. Bee venom. Junior swears by it for his arthritis. Says bee venom is the best kind of ointment to put on his sore and swollen joints."

Elizabeth laughed, shaking her head. "I'll pass, thank you. Unless you guys just happen to come upon some bee venom tomorrow in your search for Mary Chamblis." Her eyes lit up. "Now that you mention bees, I would love to have some natural honey to go in my herb tea."

Michael shook his head. "Don't think we'll be robbing any bees of their venom or their honey. Sorry."

"I'll get you some honey, Elizabeth," Ben promised. "I know a fellow who does well with his bees, and his sourwood honey is the best in the mountains."

"Sourwood?" Elizabeth looked doubtful.

"The sourwood tree is considered one of the best bee trees. That's where Mr. Foster gets his honey, and believe me, it's so popular the shops in Angel Valley can't keep it stocked."

"Then I'd like to try it. Thanks for thinking of it, Ben. That's awfully sweet."

"My pleasure." He looked from Elizabeth back to Michael. "See you at seven in the morning, Michael."

Michael opened the door for him and watched as he bounded off to his truck. He glanced over his shoulder. "Ben's quite a guy, isn't he?"

"Yes, he is. But Michael," she sighed, "I'm afraid I won't be able to concentrate on my reading while you're gone."

"Why is that?"

"Because I'll be worrying about you and Ben sneaking around dangerous territory."

Michael was watching Ben drive away, but at those words he turned and walked back to sit down beside his wife. "I don't want you worrying." He rubbed her sore leg. "I want you to rest up tomorrow so you'll be ready for some fun during the rest of our stay."

Elizabeth took a deep breath and placed a loving hand on Michael's shoulder. "Just being with you is fun, darling. I love it."

Michael awoke just before six and peered through the semi-darkness at the clock by the bed. This was his usual waking-up time back at Oak Shadows, so he knew his system must be getting back on a routine again. His head rolled on the pillow, and he looked across at Elizabeth, snuggled into the pillow. Sometime during the night she had turned on her side, facing the opposite wall. That made it easier for him to gently slip out of bed.

Quietly he opened the closet door and removed a clean pair of jeans and a heavy sweater from the hangers. Then he opened a drawer, pulled out underwear and socks, and then reached down for his hiking boots. With everything in hand, he tiptoed out of the bedroom, quietly closing the door behind him. He went to the smaller guest bedroom to dress; then he hurried to the kitchen and put on a pot of coffee.

While waiting for the coffee to perk, he walked to the sliding glass doors. As quietly as possible he unlocked the door and slipped out onto the deck. The crisp morning air was invigorating, nipping at his face and sending out a challenge for the day. He shoved his hands into the back pockets of his jeans and looked toward the east.

A new day was forming out on the horizon as a sliver of gray light began to penetrate the soft darkness. Narrowing his eyes, he could vaguely see the tips of the mountain peaks, soaring and majestic, older than time. Suddenly he felt touched to the core of his being by the beauty that God had created here in the Smokies. He sank into the porch chair and said a silent prayer, for Katie back home, for his parents, and for his brother,

Jay, Jay's wife, Tracy, and their daughter, Brooke. *And please help us on this search, God. We need to find Mary Chamblis.*

Just as he finished his prayer, he heard the engine of a truck climbing up the drive past the chalets. The headlights of the truck cast twin spots of yellow into the grayness of early morning. Michael sat waiting as Ben's truck slowly approached and turned in before the chalet.

He stood smiling, waiting for Ben to hop out of his truck. In the first light of morning he could see that Ben was carrying a small sack in his hands as he hurried up the porch steps. He, too, was dressed in jeans and hiking boots, a sweater, and a light windbreaker.

"Had breakfast?" Ben grinned at him.

"No, but I have the coffee. Come on in. Elizabeth is still asleep."

"Glad you warned me. Mom used to say I could wake up the entire household simply by walking down the hall."

Michael chuckled softly as they entered the chalet and went to the kitchen. He pulled down two large mugs and filled them with coffee while Ben opened the sack and removed two huge biscuits with thick slabs of sausage tucked inside. "Compliments of my landlady at the boarding house where I stay. She isn't supposed to provide food, but she's up bright and early every morning, and I don't think I've ever left there on an empty stomach. She's great!"

"She appreciates a good boarder." Michael grinned as he got napkins and accepted his breakfast from Ben. "Hey, this biscuit is the size of a pancake," he said, gripping it with both hands.

"She cooks for one of the big restaurants in Pigeon Forge. I really lucked out when I snagged a room in her house!"

"You certainly did," Michael agreed, upon tasting the biscuit.

They munched happily, sipping the strong black coffee and watching the morning grow brighter beyond the kitchen window. When they had finished their sausage-and-biscuit breakfast and drained the coffee mugs, Michael cleaned up and grabbed a couple of apples. "In case we get hungry." He tossed one of the apples to Ben.

"Thanks. I carry those little cheese-and-cracker packs with me all the time. So we're in good shape." Ben tapped the jacket of his pocket and something rustled in response.

They slipped out of the chalet, and Michael carefully locked the door behind them. Michael could see Ben's truck more clearly now. It looked as though it had successfully climbed many a mountain, judging from the mud on its fenders.

"Want to tackle that old forestry road first?" Michael asked as their hiking boots crunched over the graveled drive.

"I thought of that, but here's my suggestion," Ben said as they climbed into his truck. "We could park at Painted Rock, get out, and find that trail Millie told you about. I got the map out and went over it again last night. I figured out how we can hike around the lower ledge of that mountain and come out just up the valley from the Stringfellow property. It's a steep up-and-down trail, but its the quickest way to get there if you're up to it."

Michael nodded. "I think I'm up to it. At least, I'll give it my best effort."

Ben grinned at his response. "Then if we don't find anything that interests you around the Stringfellow property, we can turn and hit the trail east. It leads several miles on and finally ends up in Cherokee."

Michael listened, nodding his head. "Sounds like a good plan, Ben. I can see you're going to be a great help to me."

As Ben started up the engine, Michael noticed how well

equipped Ben was for his lifestyle here in the mountains. Looking through the glass window to the bed of the truck, Michael spotted a neat coil of rope, a shovel, an ax, and a toolbox. In the cab of the truck, there was the forestry map, along with a compass and a clean towel on the seat.

"You seem to have thought of everything," Michael observed after glancing around. "Guess you're used to the lifestyle here."

Ben nodded, putting the gearshift into drive. Beneath the thick blond hair, which had no particular style but simply fell into casual waves about his face, his eyes flashed with adventure.

"I've put a lot of thought into the time I spend here," Ben said. "I had a few mishaps at first and learned the hard way what you don't leave home without. Incidentally, I have a canteen of water back there too." He indicated the back of the truck.

"A true mountain man," Michael commended him.

As they drove along, Ben shifted gears easily and cast his eyes toward the mountains. "I love it here," he said. "After I finish up my thesis, I'd like to come back and settle somewhere around this area."

"Sounds good to me. What are you planning to do?"

"I want to write a book about the people here. The mountaineers, the Cherokees, and the neighborly way of life in Pigeon Forge, Gatlinburg, and Angel Valley. They're always so happy, so pleasant, so...real."

Michael nodded. "I know what you mean. I've sensed that too. Tell me about the book you want to write, Ben."

"Well..." Ben hesitated, glancing at Michael. "You sure you want to get me started on the subject? I tend to bore some people with it."

"You won't bore me," Michael assured him.

"Stop me if I do. My plan is to first find another job to support myself and moonlight with my writing. I could always teach since I'll have my master's next spring, but I would be willing to do any kind of work just for the privilege of being here. As for my book, the legends and lore that I'm gathering have been a dream of mine for years. During my twelfth summer my parents brought my sister and me here on a two-week vacation from Chicago, our home town. I'll tell you, this place made a lasting impression on me. I already knew I wanted to go to school in the South because I was tired of the hustle and bustle of Chicago. We spent a night in Knoxville, near the University of Tennessee campus, and that cinched it for me. Two other summers I came back and hiked around these valleys and mountains as much as I could. When I got accepted at UT and came to school here, I majored in journalism and minored in geography. It's worked out just right for me," he said with a grin of satisfaction as he steered the wheel along the winding road with ease. It was obvious he was practiced at handling his truck on tricky curves.

"No girlfriends?" Michael asked, sure there must have been some.

"One or two," Ben conceded. "But I haven't met my soul mate yet."

"Soul mate," Michael said on a sigh. "That's a great way to describe it. And don't settle for less." As the truck climbed the mountain to Painted Rock, Michael thought about his years with Elizabeth. "You know, making a commitment isn't easy, but I can honestly tell you that when you find the right person, the person who completes you, it's one of God's greatest blessings."

"I can see you two have that." Ben spoke softly, turning into the parking area at Painted Rock. He looked across at Michael, genuinely interested in what he had to say.

"Yep, we're soul mates, as you said."

For a moment Michael's thoughts drifted back to some of the more painful times of their marriage, when they were both learning the rules of give-and-take in their relationship. He was tempted to share this with Ben, but then he decided against it. The problems he and Elizabeth had had in trying to adjust and build a happy marriage belonged to a private place in their hearts.

Ben cut the engine of the truck, and they both looked around. No other vehicles had arrived this early, and yet it was the perfect time of morning. The sunlight was becoming brighter, touching the tops of the spruce, fir, and pine trees on the mountains. Adding to that beauty was the way the mountains formed layers against the horizon while a curl of mist settled over the valley below. He recalled what Wyn had said about Mary's comparing the mist to spirits. Maybe when he finally found her, he and Elizabeth could share their belief in the one true Spirit.

Ben was reaching for his windbreaker, and Michael pulled his thoughts back to the present as he got out of the truck. While Ben locked the truck, Michael walked over to the lookout, studying it thoughtfully. He turned to Ben, approaching him. "That's a long way down," he said, shaking his head.

"Yes, it is," Ben agreed, looking into the vastness below them.

"Ben, it seems to me if Mary Chamblis had fallen, someone would have heard her scream. It's also hard to believe that the search-and-rescue unit didn't locate her body if she fell."

"Yeah, it's puzzling isn't it?" Ben frowned.

Studying him, Michael grinned, shoving his hands into the

pockets of his thick sweater. "You know something, Ben? Among your other talents you just might turn out to be a decent detective as well. Knowing your turf, as they say in Atlanta, is the first step."

Ben laughed softly as they set off over the trail he had described earlier. It was a still, quiet morning, with only the occasional crunch of their footsteps over broken twigs to break the silence. Occasionally a small animal scampered farther back into the underbrush. The men were quiet as they walked along, moving deeper into the wilderness.

The air felt cold on Michael's cheeks, and he bunched his shoulders together, walking faster. Just as Ben had pointed out, the trail was as crooked as a snake, curving, winding, plunging deeper into the woods. Checking his watch, Michael noted that they had been walking briskly for almost an hour before the trail widened and opened onto a summit.

They stopped to catch their breath, both winded from the steep incline they had just covered. Michael lifted the binoculars and peered down into the valley. Although the tree cover was heavy, he could see the distant outline of an old frame house, badly in need of paint, with smoke curling up from its brick chimney. The house was in a private cove surrounded by small patches of woods, and far to the rear he could distinguish a garden of some kind.

"Can you see the Stringfellow house?" Ben asked.

Michael handed him the binoculars. Ben looked through the lens and began to nod. "Yep, that's the place. There's nobody outside this early. Wait, someone just came out."

He handed the binoculars back to Michael. Michael spotted a rotund, red-faced fellow in overalls, standing on the front porch, looking right to left. Soon a black-and-white hound loped around the side of the house and began to bark.

Even from a distance the harsh bellow of the man echoed down the valley as he scolded the dog. In immediate response the dog slunk back around the far side of the house.

"Let's just hang out here for a little while and watch them," Michael suggested, dropping to sit cross-legged on the ground. "I welcome the chance to catch my breath, don't you?"

"Right," Ben said, kneeling down and leaning back against a tree, his feet stretched out before him. He squinted down toward the cabin. "I'm in no hurry to go calling; I can tell you that for sure."

Presently the big fellow went back inside the house and slammed the door. Michael studied the house. It appeared to have five or six rooms, with a porch that had been braced over the years. He pondered the possibilities of what to do. After a while he looked at Ben.

"Well, why don't we mosey down there and ask directions?"

Ben's hazel eyes widened. "We'd better ask for more than directions. They know you don't just happen upon their place for no reason. I mean, it isn't feasible that someone would hike several miles over that rough trail with no objective in mind." His brow furrowed as he squinted down at the Stringfellow property. "Wait a minute. I see some sourwood trees. We were just talking about honey. I seem to remember Millie saying something about the Stringfellow woman bringing in honey to one of the shops."

Michael's expression brightened. "Elizabeth wants honey for her tea. Let's give it a try."

Ben took a deep breath. "Okay, but don't get too close to the house, and be prepared to make a hasty exit. That guy Buster already ran me off once before I could even tell him what I wanted."

"Then I'll tell him straight out that we came to buy honey."

"And you'd better talk fast," Ben said, as they made their way down the sloping trail to the property.

"I can do that," Michael assured him.

They were still sixty yards from the house, but in plain view, when the big man stepped out on the porch again, shotgun in hand.

"We want to buy some sourwood honey," Michael called out. "Lots of it."

The man lumbered down the porch steps and started walking in their direction. "Hold it right there," he yelled, eyeing them suspiciously.

He was somewhere in his thirties, although it was difficult for Michael to guess his age. A baseball cap was jammed on his blond head, the bill lowered over his brow. His face was as round as a dinner plate, his features thick, his neck wide. He wore a red checkered flannel shirt under a pair of faded overalls. And his eyes were narrowing to slits as he came closer to them, looking from one to the other.

He scowled at Ben. "You been here before."

"Yes, sir. I never got a chance to talk to you."

Michael jumped into the conversation before it went any further. "I'm from Atlanta," he said. "I'm helping Wyn Dalton look for his missing fiancée, Mary Chamblis. She's a pretty blond woman in her midtwenties—"

"Buster Stringfellow," he said, cocking the rifle. "And I ain't seen her."

"Okay, what about the honey? My wife heard that you people have the best sourwood honey around. Can I buy some?"

Buster frowned at him, sending thick furrows over his forehead. "Depends on how much you want. Won't be robbing the hives again till tonight."

"Oh, I want as much as you'll sell," Michael offered quickly, taking another step toward Buster. "After all, we can't buy sourwood honey in Atlanta, and my wife loves it."

Buster was obviously thinking this over as he glared at Michael, but his hand relaxed on the shotgun.

"Come back in a couple of days," he barked. "That all?"

Michael took a deep breath. This was obviously as far as they were going to get. He cast one last glance toward the house. His vibes just didn't tell him that Mary Chamblis was inside.

"That's all," he said, shoving his hands back in his pockets. "Thanks. Ready, Ben?"

"I'm ready," Ben said hoarsely.

Michael turned and began to walk away, hoping Buster wouldn't change his mind and use the shotgun. Ben took a few steps backwards, as though not so sure of it, then turned and joined Michael.

When they were out of earshot, Ben pointed toward the woods.

"We can cut through those woods, hit the trail east toward Cherokee if you want."

"Might as well," Michael said, unable to keep the disappointment from his voice.

After they had trudged a quarter of a mile, Michael ventured a glance back toward the old house. Buster had gone inside. If they were holding Mary captive, it made sense that he would wait on the porch to be sure they were out of sight. But they could watch from the window just as well.

"What do you think?" Ben glanced at Michael as they trudged wearily through the woods.

"I don't know. I guess I don't think she's there."

"Then we'll keep a lookout for—" he cleared his throat— "a body along this trail. I don't know how or why she would have come this far, but—"

"But we explore every possibility," Michael said with a heavy sigh. "It's all we can do."

Michael thought of Elizabeth. He longed to be with her, instead of trudging through the back trails of the Smoky Mountains. He stared down at his worn hiking boots, wondering how long he and Ben had been walking. He began to suspect they were hopelessly lost.

Suddenly Ben nudged him. "Look!"

Michael lifted his head and squinted through the sunlight. Just ahead, a quaint log cabin nestled on the edge of the woods. The cabin appeared to be occupied. An old rocking chair sat on the porch, and calico curtains framed the windows. Slowly the door opened, and both men stopped walking as a young woman stepped out. She was dressed in tan doeskin with matching moccasins, and her dark hair was plaited neatly in braids on each side of her face.

Michael rubbed his weary eyes and blinked. "Is she real, or did we just fall back into the last century?"

Ben's voice was low and gentle, the tone he used when trying not to frighten a creature of the woods. "Either she's real, or she's our guardian angel. Either way, she's the most beautiful woman I've ever seen."

FIVE

ichael was the first to regain his senses. "She doesn't look unfriendly." He nudged Ben. "Let's go talk with her."

She watched them carefully, saying nothing as they slowly approached. Ben was the first to call out to her.

"Hi. I'm Ben Thornton, and this is Michael Calloway. Michael is an investigator, and I'm a graduate student at UT in Knoxville. Could we talk with you for a minute?"

She closed the door behind her and sat down in the rocking chair, brushing a sweep of dark bangs across her forehead. "A minute," she replied in a soft, low voice.

Michael moved faster than Ben, who seemed to be transfixed by her even though he had been the first to speak. Michael noted that she was an attractive woman. Her complexion was lighter than the other Cherokee women he had met, but she had dark eyes and black hair that gleamed in the morning light.

They had approached her porch steps by now. Ben was staring at the tan doeskin dress with deep fringe extending from the long sleeves.

Michael removed the picture of Mary Chamblis from his pocket. "We're looking for this young woman who disappeared from Painted Rock," he began, showing her the picture.

"Painted Rock's a long way from here," she said slowly, measuring both men with her dark eyes.

"Yes, it is," Michael agreed. "But the search-and-rescue unit has combed that area and found no sign of her."

She nodded. "They came here too, but I'll tell you what I told them. There's been no blond woman at my door, or anyone accompanying her." She did not reach for the picture to study it as most people did. "I already saw the flyer with her picture in Cherokee," she said, looking at Michael.

"Well," Michael said, reaching into his pocket and removing his business card, "may I leave this with you in case you hear anything about her? Or on the off chance that you should see her?"

She accepted the card, studying it thoughtfully. "You're all the way from Atlanta?"

"Yes, I've been hired by her fiancé to help the police locate her. So far, they've had no luck in finding her."

"I see." She glanced up at him. Her fingers closed over the card. "If I see Mary Chamblis, I will ask her to contact you."

Michael caught the underlying meaning of her words. Not *I will contact you; I will ask her to contact you.* He knew this woman was giving Mary a break in case she didn't want to be found.

"Thanks." His eyes moved to the front of the cabin. "Do you live alone, may I ask?"

"Yes, I do. My parents are dead," she said, her voice still soft yet reserved. "The reason I'm dressed like this—" she lifted the arm of the dress, and the fringe rippled—"is because I design clothes for a shop in Cherokee."

"That's a beautiful dress," Ben said, his eyes wide as he looked at her. It was obvious to Michael that Ben was quite taken with her.

She looked Ben over but did not return his smile. "Thank you. I was trying it on for size when I saw you approaching."

Silence fell over the group before Michael cleared his throat.

He wished he could get a look at the inside of the cabin, although he had no doubt that she was telling the truth. "What is your name, by the way?"

"I'm Raven," she said.

"Raven." Ben repeated the name as he edged closer, obviously fascinated.

She nodded, still studying him thoughtfully.

"Raven, I'm doing a study on the people of this region, and I'm particularly interested in the Cherokees. I'd love to visit with you sometime, learn more about your way of life."

A tiny smile touched her lips. She wore no makeup, yet she was striking with the gleaming dark hair and deep thoughtful brown eyes. "What would you like to know?"

Michael's lips quirked in amusement. She had a way of pinning a person, forcing you to get to the point. Turning to his friend, he watched Ben squirm slightly beneath her steady gaze.

"Well, for starters, I guess I'm just curious about why a young woman like you would want to live out here all alone. And how long have you lived here?"

"The cabin has always been my home, although I went out to school for a while, then came back." Her eyes slipped over their heads to the surrounding hills. "I do not care for city life. I only go to Cherokee now."

"I see," Ben said, openly staring.

Michael cleared his throat. "How far from here into Cherokee?"

"If you follow this trail," she said, pointing, "you will hit a wide road that leads straight into the reservation. From right here, it's about three miles into the reservation."

Michael nodded, looking around. He didn't see a vehicle and wondered if she walked back and forth. It seemed like they had stepped into a time machine and been whisked back to another generation, although he could see from the cabin and grounds that the woman was poor.

"Well, Ben." Michael turned to nudge him. "Shall we head on and see what we can find out?"

Ben dragged his eyes from Raven and looked at Michael. "Er, sure." Then instantly his gaze shot back to Raven. "Could we drop by again sometime? Or could I? I'd love to interview you for the thesis I'm doing for school."

She nodded. "I'm in Cherokee every Friday and Saturday. I could see you there."

She gave him the name of the shop and the address, and Michael jotted both down in his notebook. He wasn't sure Ben would remember; he had never seen anyone so impressed.

Michael closed the notebook and returned it to his pocket. "It was nice meeting you, Raven."

"Thank you. I wish you luck with your search."

"Her fiancé is really worried about her," he emphasized.

She nodded slowly. "I'm sure he is. But many people have disappeared in these mountains."

Her eyes drifted upward to the sprawling mountain range.

"Thanks again," Ben said, finally regaining his composure and turning to Michael. "Ready to set off on the trail again?"

"Ready if you are." Michael grinned at him.

"Good-bye," they called in unison.

Raven murmured a soft good-bye and followed them with her eyes. When they were at a comfortable distance, Ben turned to Michael. "That's the way these people are. They're very reserved and a bit skeptical of strangers."

"She's a pretty woman. You noticed that, didn't you?"

He turned to Michael with wide eyes. "She was the most beautiful woman I've ever seen."

Michael slapped him good-naturedly on the shoulder. "Careful. You may lose your heart and forget about that thesis you're supposed to write."

Ben shook his head. "I would love to interview her. Think of the knowledge she could give me about her people."

"Yep," Michael agreed absently. His thoughts were already on the trail ahead. Unlike the miles of dense, overgrown paths they had covered, this trail had been traveled. Despite the heavy tree cover, the path had begun to widen. It broke into a clearing thirty yards ahead, as Raven had told them..

Both men lengthened their stride, dispensing with conversation. The two-mile stretch into Cherokee was uneventful as far as seeing any other cabins or finding any more clues to Mary Chamblis, as far as Michael was concerned.

Ben, however, seemed to have gotten his second wind. "That's the Oconaluftee River." He pointed to the river that paralleled the road.

Michael glanced toward the clear water. "My brother Jay would love to be casting into that river for a trout. What's the limit here?"

Ben frowned. "Maybe ten a day. I don't know. I never take the time to fish, although I probably should. This is prime fishing. We are now on the reservation," he said, lifting an arm to indicate the area around them. "This is the Qualla Boundary, about fifty-six thousand acres that was held in trust by the federal government for the eastern band of Cherokees."

Michael perked up a bit, studying the shops they were approaching. Through the glass windows he could see displays of Native American crafts and art. "Elizabeth would love this," he said, thinking of her again. "I'm going to call her to come get us and pray she doesn't insist on lingering to shop."

"Why don't you two come back tomorrow?"

"I doubt that my schedule will permit it." His eyes lingered on a bookstore that featured out-of-print books, and this interested him. "On second thought, maybe we will come back. I really should look around here a bit more for Mary Chamblis, I suppose." He found himself thinking not of Mary but of the Cherokee people. He glanced at Ben and saw that he was intently studying the bookstore as well.

"I read about the Trail of Tears," Michael said. "What a sad experience."

"Yeah," Ben agreed. "I've always had a special sympathy for the Native Americans. They're such a brave and noble people."

The first eating place loomed just ahead, and Michael almost moaned with relief as he and Ben exchanged grins of satisfaction. "I'll call Elizabeth from here and ask her to drive over and pick us up. I can't walk another yard!" Michael groaned. His legs were aching, his back was tired, and he already had a blister on his right toe even though his hiking boots had been quite comfortable before today. "Think my feet must be swelling a bit."

Ben nodded. "That's what happens when you first start hiking a lot before you become accustomed to it. I'm all for a ride if you think your wife won't mind."

"She won't mind. You just snag us a comfortable seat inside," Michael said, hobbling toward the pay phone outside the restaurant. After he deposited the appropriate number of quarters for a call to the Angel Valley area, Elizabeth's voice came over the wire.

"Hey, hon. We're in Cherokee. We hiked all the way from Painted Rock."

"You *what*? You must be exhausted."

"Exactly. Do you feel up to driving over to pick us up?"

"Of course I do. I'm already getting cabin fever."

"Okay. Just ask the office manager the directions for getting over here, or check out the map. When you pass the bridge over the river and come through a traffic light, we're at the first restaurant on the right."

"I'll leave in just a few minutes. You guys just stay put."

"I don't think we can do anything else," he groaned. "Thanks, darling. Love you."

Michael hobbled back inside to face Ben with a triumphant smile. "Our ride has graciously agreed to come for us. But we might as well kick back. It'll be a while."

"I didn't think we were capable of doing anything *but* kick back." Ben grinned.

Michael collapsed into the booth again. "You see. You need a soul mate."

"Uh-huh." Ben's eyes lifted over Michael's head, staring absently at the wall. "I want to get to know Raven better."

"Aha! Smitten already," Michael teased.

Ben shrugged. "I told you, mountain people and Native Americans interest me very much."

"Then you're definitely doing your research in the right location!"

Elizabeth had no trouble finding the restaurant or Michael, facing the door. He was slumped in a booth, his legs stretched out on the seat and extending into the aisle, his dark head pressed against the wall as he softly snored. Ben, sitting opposite him, merely grinned at her and sat there, looking perfectly content.

She chuckled to herself, trying to imagine her husband playing Daniel Boone, tramping up and down the mountains with a pro like Ben.

"He flaked out on you, huh?"

"He was a good trooper. We've walked miles and miles."

Elizabeth smiled at Ben and leaned over to plant a kiss on her husband's parted lips. He stirred, dark lashes opened slowly, then snapped wide. He stared into her eyes, then bolted up and looked around, self-consciously.

"Hi, Daniel Boone," she said, pushing his feet off the leather seat so she could sit down.

He grinned sleepily. "I must be in heaven. You are an angel, aren't you?"

Elizabeth's eyes glowed with amusement as she glanced down at her sweatshirt and jeans, looked across at Ben, then back at Michael. "An angel in blue jeans, that's me."

"Are you hungry?" Ben thought to ask.

"No, but what about you guys?"

"We pigged out on giant hamburgers and French fries while we waited."

She nodded. "Did you find out anything about Mary?"

Michael groaned as he reached for his coffee mug. "Don't even ask."

"Then I'll ask Ben," she answered coolly, focusing her brown eyes on Ben.

"I can tell you what we did learn. We learned that the Stringfellows will let you half a mile close to their property if you order a dozen gallons of sourwood honey, which your husband did."

"What?" She whirled to Michael, who merely shook his head.

"And we learned that a beautiful Cherokee woman lives in a cabin just a few miles out of Cherokee."

"Oh?" She hiked a brow and turned to Michael.

"Her name is Raven, and Ben's been addled every since he saw her."

Elizabeth's lips curved upward in a pleased little smile. "Hmm. That sounds interesting."

"Can we go home now?" Michael asked, slipping his arm around her shoulder.

"Well, if I'm merely to be the chauffeur, then I'll expect a hefty tip for the ride."

"You'll get one," Michael promised, wrinkling his nose at her.

As they started out of the restaurant, Ben began to chuckle. "You two make quite a pair. Elizabeth still has a bit of a limp on the right side, and you, Michael, look as though you should be dragged to the car, instead of trying to walk on your own."

"If we look that suspicious, your reputation may be at stake, Ben," Elizabeth teased, as they climbed into the Blazer. "I take it I'm to do the driving. No male chauvinists here."

"None here," Michael sighed. He fell into the passenger's side while Ben crawled gratefully into the backseat.

"Well, in that case, I don't want any coaching on my driving skills."

"You'll hear no complaints from me," Ben promised. "If I can just be delivered to my truck at Painted Rock, I will be very, very grateful."

"I think I can do that," Elizabeth said, nodding.

By the time she turned the key in the ignition and switched on the headlights, Michael was snoring again.

SIX

Tell me all about it!" Elizabeth sat propped against the pillows, snuggled into her robe.

She had allowed Michael to have the sole comfort of the Jacuzzi to try to ease the ache from his tortured muscles.

"Tell you about what?" he called to her. "It wasn't my best day; I can promise you that."

She could hear the splash of water as he dragged himself out of the Jacuzzi. "In fact, I'm beginning to wonder if this case can be solved," he added miserably.

"Come on. You never give up easily. You're just worn out. After a good night's rest, you'll be ready to tackle this case again first thing in the morning."

He entered the bedroom, buttoning the shirt of his pajamas. "What I don't want to tackle is Buster Stringfellow. That guy is about the size of Ben's truck."

He sank onto the bed beside her and carefully lifted his legs. "The Jacuzzi and aspirin definitely helped," he said with a deep sigh. "Ah, the comforts of home."

"Michael." She lifted his hand to her mouth to kiss his fingers; then her eyes grew serious. "I want you to be very careful traipsing around the back country. I love you so much. I don't want to lose you again."

"You're not going to lose me," he teased, leaning forward to give her a kiss of reassurance. "Do you want to hear how Raven knocked the socks off Ben? Well, not literally," he added, as Elizabeth's eyes widened.

She laughed. "Of course I want to hear! Tell me."

Michael began with his first impression of Raven standing on the porch of her log cabin. He told her everything, even the part about Ben's inviting himself back.

"I want to meet her," Elizabeth said, her eyes twinkling with delight. "Maybe you and I can play Cupid for Ben."

Michael chuckled. "I don't think we'll have to do that. Ben seems to be doing okay on his own."

"How did she respond to him?" Elizabeth asked, eager to hear more.

Michael stared into space, recalling the exchange between them. "She's very reserved, but Ben says that's the way most of the mountain people are, and the Native Americans as well. And yet she was polite to Ben; she didn't seem to object to his coming back to see her again, although she suggested he come to her place of employment in Cherokee."

"That's the shop where she markets the dresses she designs?"

"Right, and—"

The telephone rang, interrupting their speculation on a romance for Ben.

"Oh, I'll bet that's Wyn Dalton." Elizabeth frowned. "I forgot to tell you, but he called earlier. Just wanted to know if you were making any progress."

Michael reached for the phone on the table beside the bed. As he answered, he nodded at Elizabeth. "Hi, Wyn. I've spent the past two days exploring all the coves and valleys around Painted Rock. In fact today Ben Thornton and I followed the trail that forks back east all the way to Cherokee."

Michael paused, listening, then he began to explain who Ben was. He shook his head, taking a deep breath. "I'm sorry to report that, so far, I've been unable to turn up anything you don't already know, Wyn."

Michael looked at Elizabeth, rolling his eyes, while Wyn replied. "Yes, I understand that. And I've made everyone aware of the reward, but it doesn't seem to help." He paused to grab a breath. "We even went onto the Stringfellow property today. They're reputed to be the meanest people in the mountains. From what we could see, there was no sign of Mary there. But I'm not ruling that possibility out." He nodded again. "I'll keep you informed."

He hung up and shook his head. "The poor guy may be getting his hopes up for nothing. If she's inside that house, she's well hidden. We watched the place from the top of the mountain for over an hour. I never saw a woman anywhere. That doesn't mean she isn't inside, but my instincts just don't lead me in that direction anymore. For one thing, if she were there, I think she could have somehow managed to escape by now."

"But you did go on the property?"

"Halfway. That's when we met up with Buster. Thank God, Ben came up with the idea of getting that honey for you. Buster responded to that. Said to come back in a couple of days. They have to rob the hives first. I'll feel sorrier for the bees than for those guys."

"I just don't think she's there either," Elizabeth said, staring into space. "Something about that doesn't feel right."

"I know. The other possibility is the van that Wyn spotted." He turned to a small table where he had stacked several files. He withdrew one and opened it up. "The sheriff thinks these people are harmless, but maybe he's wrong. I may have to drive down to Birmingham and check them out." He looked over the folder to Elizabeth, who was already grimacing.

"Wait a minute," she said, folding her arms over her chest. "Since Jay is in Atlanta and closer to Birmingham than we are, why not ask Jay to check them out? Then if he thinks it's necessary, we could drive down there."

He laid the folder on the table and returned to the sofa. "We?" he repeated, tweaking her cheek as he stretched out beside her.

"Yes, *we*. I'm as interested in this case as you are."

Michael nodded. "I believe you are." He was thoughtful for a moment. "As for asking Jay to drive to Birmingham and check these people out, that's asking a lot."

She grinned. "What are brothers for? Anyway, you could always call and ask," she suggested softly, pointing to the telephone.

He looked back at her, an amused glint in his eyes. "You know, you're getting pretty smart at this."

"I've observed the best," she quipped.

Michael glanced at his watch. "It's nine o'clock. Jay and Tracy have probably put little Brooke to bed and are settled onto the sofa. I'll give them a call."

He dialed the number and waited, then smiled across at Elizabeth. "Hey, Jay. How's my favorite little niece?"

He chuckled. "I can tell she already has you wrapped around that tiny finger of hers. Tracy doing okay?…That's good. Listen, Jay, I was wondering if I could ask a favor."

He began to update him on the case, and he told them about the Fishers in Birmingham.

"The sheriff here has talked with them and feels they're in the clear, but I'd really like to get your feelings about them." He hesitated as Jay spoke. Then Michael reached for the file on the coffee table. "Yeah, I have it right here."

He gave the Fishers' full names and their address in Bessemer. He also repeated the name of the company where the guy worked.

"Jay, I really appreciate it. I'll owe you one.…The fishing?"

Michael looked across at Elizabeth and grinned. "Yeah, there's a stream out back of us, but, no, I haven't tried to snag a trout yet. Maybe you can bring Tracy and Brooke up next summer." He smiled at Jay's reply. "Okay, I appreciate whatever you can do. Yeah, I'll be here tomorrow night." He gave him the telephone number, thanked him again, and hung up.

"Maybe my luck is finally changing," he said, winking at Elizabeth. "Jay needs to make a trip to Birmingham to check on another case, and he said tomorrow would be a good day for him to go. He'll check these people out and give me a call tomorrow night."

"Wonderful! And what did he say about little Brooke? What an adorable baby!"

"Oh, he said Brooke is absolutely terrific. Jay really sounds happy," Michael added, resting his back against the pillows and smiling contentedly as he thought of his brother's little family.

Elizabeth leaned her head on Michael's shoulder. "I was really worried about Tracy when that guy grabbed her and held her hostage for that awful Dr. Phillips."

"In the hope of stalling Jay's search for Dr. Phillips," Michael continued the thought, then reached over and took her hand. "Hey, let's not think about the bad times. I have a surprise." He reached over and opened the dresser drawer, withdrawing a chocolate candy bar for each of them, which he had deposited there the day before.

Elizabeth laughed. It was a game of theirs, surprising each other with their favorite treats. They shared a moment of laughter; then Elizabeth grew serious. "God has been so good to us, Michael."

"I know. I feel a little guilty not being in church since today is Sunday."

She nodded. "I was reading Psalms earlier. Maybe we could

have our own little devotion." She glanced toward the glass window. Through the darkness, her eyes traced the curve of the mountains against a black velvet sky. "What a beautiful place to praise God." She looked back at Michael, and her eyes were filled with love. "Oh, Michael, we really should be counting our blessings."

He nodded, wrapping his arms around her. "I know. Every morning when I wake up with you beside me, I thank God." He cupped her chin and tilted her head back to look into her eyes. "Speaking of blessings, I thought you wanted to add one."

Then he kissed her tenderly, and she remembered their conversation about having another baby.

"Yes, I do want to add another blessing. That is, if God thinks we're worthy." She wrapped her arms around his neck and pulled his lips to hers.

SEVEN

"Michael, I have an idea," Elizabeth said as they shared an early breakfast of sweet rolls, juice, and coffee. "Why don't we drive down to Knoxville and nose around? If Wyn would give us a key to Mary's apartment, we could do a little snooping and—who knows? We might come up with something that would shed some light on this situation." She shrugged as Michael studied her thoughtfully. "Well, it couldn't hurt, could it?"

"No, it couldn't," Michael answered. "I was thinking of driving down to the corporate office to speak with some of her coworkers. Even though Wyn might not want to believe it, there may be some business involvement in this. Maybe he stepped on the wrong toes, or maybe someone had been keeping an eye on Mary. Who knows? There's one thing for sure. We're not accomplishing anything sitting here."

"So what are we waiting for?"

Michael guided his Blazer along the busy interstate leading into Knoxville as Elizabeth spread a city map across her lap. "You've marked the location for Dalton Chemicals here." She pointed to the highlighted area on the map.

"Yeah, it's on the east side of Knoxville, so we'll be getting off in—" he glanced down at the map—"about three exits, I think."

"How do you maintain such a great sense of direction?"

Elizabeth asked, shaking her head. "You amaze me."

"No, darling, I just rely on maps," he said as they exited the ramp and began to search for the correct street.

They had no problem locating Dalton Chemicals, a modern office building with tinted windows and a constant array of people coming and going through the revolving doors. A spacious parking lot adjacent to the building should have provided plenty of parking space, but even so, Michael had to search to find an empty spot.

"Well, looks like business is booming here," Elizabeth remarked, noting all the cars.

"Yep. It's a well-known company, and they do an amazing amount of business. They have offices in New York and Los Angeles as well."

"And where, exactly, does Wyn Dalton fit into the family plan of Dalton Chemicals?"

"He's heir apparent to the fortune even though his father is chairman of the board and his uncle holds a seat on the board of directors. But apparently Wyn has done a good job in running the company. He's been written up in several articles as the rising young executive to watch."

Elizabeth sighed. "Well, apparently someone was watching him pretty closely and figured out he could pay a very hefty ransom."

Michael parked the Blazer and cut the engine, then looked across at her. "Then why hasn't that someone contacted him?"

She chewed her lip. "Maybe he's biding his time for one reason or another. The answer to this mysterious case has to be the money, Michael."

He nodded, pocketing his keys. "That's exactly what I'm thinking. Well, shall we go in and snoop around?"

Elizabeth laughed. "I love doing this. I get to apply all my years of psychological evaluation in observing people!"

They crossed the parking lot and entered single file through the revolving doors into an atrium lobby where polished floors did not show signs of the heavy traffic. The woman behind the huge oval reception center seemed unperturbed by the busy day.

"Good morning," Michael said, as they approached. "I would like to see Wyn Dalton, if possible. I don't have an appointment, but—"

"You don't?" She was a striking brunette in her midthirties, who dressed as though she had just returned from a fashion show in Paris. Her sleek black hair was short and fit her head like a small, glossy cap. Lowering her thick lashes, she consulted the huge book before her. "I'm afraid he's in meetings all day."

"Would you please tell him Michael Calloway is here? I think he'll see me, as I'm doing some special work for him concerning Mary Chamblis."

Her head jerked up, and her eyes swept Michael and darted to Elizabeth. Saying nothing more, she lifted the phone and punched in a series of numbers. She repeated the sentence to someone else and replaced the phone. "His administrative assistant asked me to direct you up to his suite. You may have to wait a few minutes," she added, as though emphasizing her disapproval of people who showed up unannounced.

"Fine. And what number is his suite?" Michael asked matter-of-factly, obviously unimpressed by her opinion.

"The fifth floor. Suite 510."

"Thank you."

He and Elizabeth hurried to the bank of elevators, and Elizabeth snickered. "Well done. She isn't quite as important as she imagines herself to be."

An elevator door slid open, and they stepped onto the tan carpet. Michael pushed number five on the keypad and the doors closed quietly. The elevator whisked them up. When they located Wyn's outer office, the receptionist here was more cordial, introducing herself as Caroline and asking them to follow her down the corridor. Three doors down Wyn was stepping into the hallway, saying good-bye to a distinguished-looking older man.

"Michael and Elizabeth," he called pleasantly. "Do come in."

They followed him inside. The office was elegant, with an end window that featured a backdrop of the Knoxville skyline.

He stood beside them, his eyes hopeful. "Do you have some news?"

Michael hesitated. It hadn't occurred to him that Wyn would interpret their arrival as breaking news. "I'm sorry to say I don't have anything, Wyn."

"Oh." His shoulders slumped as he turned and walked back to the chair behind his desk, motioning them to the armchairs opposite him.

A photo on Wyn's desk caught Michael's eye. "Is that a recent picture?" He indicated the photo of Mary that was a larger version of the face on the poster.

Wyn nodded. "It was taken two weeks before she disappeared. She planned to use it for her engagement picture, which would have been published in the newspaper." He touched the picture thoughtfully, then looked at Elizabeth and Michael.

Michael nodded. "Wyn, I thought it would be helpful to come down here today and have a look around at—"

"Look around?" Wyn's eyebrow hiked. He was obviously caught off guard.

"What I mean," Michael explained patiently, "is that I'd like to meet some of her coworkers, see if there's an off chance that someone here might have—"

"No," Wyn was shaking his head. "You're welcome to look around, but there's no reason to suspect anyone here. Our employees are carefully screened, and Mary had plenty of friends in the accounting department where she worked."

"But that's the point, Wyn. Sometimes people who pass themselves off as friends can actually have dollar signs dancing in their heads. This is obviously an impressive building, and people here know you could pay a considerable ransom for her."

Wyn stared at him. "But why wouldn't I have had a ransom call by now?"

"That may be part of the answer to the mystery. They're letting enough time lapse to throw off any suspicion that would connect Mary's disappearance to something that may have taken place recently, something you might not be aware of."

Wyn slumped deeper into the chair, staring at his desk. After a thoughtful moment, he spoke. "Well, you may have something there. I hired you to cover all the bases, so I don't want to block any progress you might make. How can I help? You want a tour of the building?"

"Just an introduction to some of her coworkers, and I'd like to have a look at her desk."

Wyn still seemed to regard the suggestion with a bit of trepidation while trying to look hopeful. "If you think it'll help."

"Let's put it this way. It can't hurt. I'd also like a key to her condominium if you don't mind. I'd like to go through it and look for anything that might give us some clue as to what's going on."

Wyn shrugged. "Sure, but I've been over there a dozen times. Nothing has changed; it's exactly as she left it."

Michael nodded. "I don't expect anything to have changed. I just want to learn more about who she was. I've learned from past experience that the better you can get to know a subject's habits, way of life, even living conditions, the easier it becomes to track that person down."

Wyn's shoulders shrugged lightly against the expensive dark suit. "Whatever you think." It was obvious he considered the plan a waste of time, and yet he offered no objection.

"Another thing," Michael inserted gently. "Do you have any business acquaintances with a personal grudge against you? Is there anyone you can think of who would abduct Mary to get back at you?"

Wyn shook his head. "I've been over that a hundred times in my head. I honestly can't think of anyone, but I'll talk to Dad again."

Michael nodded. It would be unusual for someone in Wyn's position not to have made an enemy or two along the way.

Wyn came to his feet. "Well, if you'll follow me, I'll take you down to the Accounting Department where Mary worked and introduce you to some of her coworkers."

"Thanks, Wyn. I know you're busy but—"

"I'm never too busy to find Mary," he said, leading the way to the door. "That takes top priority with me. Incidentally, would you two like a cup of coffee?"

Michael exchanged a glance with Elizabeth, and she shook her head. "No, thanks."

They returned to the bank of elevators where Wyn punched the down button. They stepped on, and the smell of his expensive cologne wafted over the interior of the elevator as he punched a lighted three on the number pad.

Michael cleared his throat. "My brother Jay, a competent investigator, is going to Birmingham to check out the Fishers again—the people in the van. He'll call me tonight."

Wyn looked at him. "Good. I'm glad you're following up on that. I admit to harboring some suspicion there. So far, those people and their mysterious van keep coming up in my mind as a distinct possibility. The sheriff seems to think they're completely harmless, but I'm not so sure about that."

"Why do you say that?" Michael pressed.

Wyn turned his pale blue eyes to Michael's curious face. "Just a hunch."

The elevator door slid back, and they stepped into a huge area of desks, ringing telephones, business machines, and computers. He led the way past workers with cluttered desks along the first aisle to an empty desk on the last row. He stood for a moment, staring at the desk, saying nothing.

The top of the desk was very neat, with only a small piece of pottery holding pens and pencils, and a carved wooden box that contained paper clips. Elizabeth was staring at the items, fascinated by what interested Mary. Pewter that she recognized from one of the shops in Angel Valley, and a handcrafted box, gleamed and polished. Impulsively Elizabeth leaned over and lifted the top of the box. Within, a blank notepad rested. She replaced the top.

Wyn had turned to the woman at the next desk. "Claire, I'd like you to meet Elizabeth and Michael Calloway. This is Claire Simpkins."

The young woman stood, looking from Michael to Elizabeth and extending her hand. She was in her late twenties, rather plain, with short brown hair, gray eyes, and a friendly smile. "How do you do?"

"They're investigating Mary's disappearance," Wyn said, lowering his voice. "They'd like to look around a bit. Will you help them?"

"Of course."

Wyn turned back to Michael. "I have a meeting in five minutes." He reached into his pocket and withdrew a key ring, then sorted through numerous keys until he located one labeled "Mary." "This is the key to Mary's apartment," he said, handing it to Michael. "Claire, can you give them instructions on how to get there since I'm about to be late for my meeting?"

She nodded quickly. "Of course."

"Sorry to intrude on you like this," Michael said. "I'll give you a call this evening."

"Thanks," Wyn replied, nodding at Elizabeth before he turned and hurried back to the elevator.

Elizabeth took a seat at the desk while Michael turned to Claire. "Did you know Mary very well?"

"Oh yes," she said, fighting back the tears that were gathering in her eyes. "I was going to be in her wedding."

Elizabeth looked at her. "Would you like to have lunch with us? Maybe we could have a more private conversation," she added, glancing around the crowded office.

Michael glanced at Elizabeth, surprised by the invitation.

Claire nodded. "Sure. I'd be happy to help in any way I can. I can't tell you how upset we've all been. If you'd like to look in Mary's desk, I have the key."

"Fine." Michael looked around the busy room. Glances were darting in their direction, while, at the same time, there was a general pretense that the appearance of two strangers at Mary's desk was nothing out of the ordinary.

Elizabeth had gotten out of the chair to give Michael access, and now her attention was centered on the various workers around the room.

Slowly, methodically, Michael went through Mary's desk, noting as he did that she was a neat, well-organized worker. All her paperwork seemed to be in order, and there was nothing in her desk to indicate that she hadn't planned to return to work on Monday as usual.

Michael closed the drawer and looked back at Claire. "Who was Mary's supervisor?"

Claire's eyes swept toward a glass-enclosed office at the rear of the long room. "Mrs. McCreary is our supervisor. She's head of accounting. Would you like to talk with her?"

When he didn't respond at once, Elizabeth glanced at Michael. He was studying a notation on a pad in her desk. He didn't seem to have heard Claire's answer.

"Michael," Elizabeth prodded, "Claire was just saying that Mrs. McCreary is Mary's supervisor. Do you want to talk with her?"

Michael still appeared deep in thought although he had turned his attention to them. "Yes, of course. Could you introduce us to Mrs. McCreary?" he asked Claire.

"Certainly."

Elizabeth noted the clock on the wall. "It's fifteen till twelve. When do you take your lunch hour, Claire?"

"Twelve is fine if that's when you'd like to go. If you'll follow me, I'll see if you can speak with Mrs. McCreary."

As they approached Mrs. McCreary's office, the tiny woman seemed to be well hidden behind a mountain of paperwork. She had bright red hair, worn very short in a style that required little care, and she was dressed in a nice burgundy suit. She appeared to be in her early fifties.

Claire knocked lightly on the door, and slowly Mrs. McCreary fought her way to eye level above the computer printouts and rolls of machine tape.

"Mrs. McCreary, Wyn Dalton brought Mr. and Mrs. Calloway up to see us. They're investigating the disappearance of Mary. Would you have a minute to speak with them?"

She looked startled but quickly recovered. "Of course. Find a chair if it's possible. We're in the middle of a tax audit, and I'm afraid my office is a disaster."

"A tax audit? Then it's a terrible time for us to intrude," Michael apologized.

She lifted a small hand, dismissing the apology. "If there's anything I could say or do to help locate poor Mary...Have you had any leads?"

Michael always hated admitting it when he had nothing to report. "We're looking into some possibilities. Today we wanted to get a feel for her work, the people she knew, her normal routine."

She nodded. "I understand."

"I gave them a key to her desk, and they looked around among her things," Claire explained.

Mrs. McCreary nodded. "It's a tragic thing for Mary to go missing, and, of course, Mr. Dalton is beside himself with worry. I have to confess it has upset me to lose a valuable worker—she was one of our best. And such a nice person to have as an employee. She never minded staying late or doing whatever was required of her. Can you think of anything that would help them, Claire?"

She shook her head. "We're going to talk some more."

Michael cleared his throat. "What I wanted to know from you, Mrs. McCreary, is..." he hesitated, trying to choose his wording. "If this seems an indelicate question, please forgive me, but as you know, I'm an investigator, and it's my job to explore every possibility. The fact that she worked in accounting and had access to lots of information about the business—"

"I see where you're leading." Mrs. McCreary's tone became

more formal. "If you're suggesting that Mary might have done anything illegal—"

"Not at all. What I'm suggesting is that she might have happened upon something in her records that would have proven disastrous to someone else. I confess it's a long shot, but as I said before, I have to consider every angle. Someone abducted this woman for a reason, and we have yet to find that reason. There's been no ransom call, so we have to assume there was another motive."

"I see." She hesitated for a moment, looking at Claire.

Claire seemed to take the hint. "I'll be at my desk if you need me. In the meantime, I'll give you a chance to talk in private." She went out and closed the door behind her.

Michael had not missed the subtle change in Mrs. McCreary's face. He suspected he had just tapped into something important, but now how did he go about gaining the woman's trust and learning the reason for the darkened expression in her eyes?

"I'm going to be very straightforward, Mrs. McCreary. In Mary's case, her life is in danger. Statistics prove that the longer a person is missing, the more likely something has happened to her."

She nodded, dropping her eyes to her hands. She had somehow managed to find a tiny vacant spot on the edge of her desk. She folded her hands on that spot and studied her short nails. "I don't know if Wyn told you this, but we had a slight discrepancy in our funds this past month."

"A slight discrepancy?"

She raised her eyes and faced him squarely. "Twenty thousand dollars is missing."

Against the background noise of ringing telephones, fingers clicking computer keys, and the constant heave of printers, the message was quite clear.

"And just what do you make of this, er, discrepancy, Mrs. McCreary?" Michael asked.

For the first time, her gray eyes reflected the weariness there, and the dark circles pronounced.

"Well, we never tally exactly to the dollar, but the most we've ever been short at the end of the month is four or five hundred dollars. This is the first time in my twenty-one years here that we've had this kind of discrepancy. And now the tax audit has all of us biting our nails."

Michael scooted to the edge of his seat. "Exactly when was this shortage noted?"

Mrs. McCreary sighed. "About two weeks before Mary disappeared. At first we thought there had been an oversight, or that we had failed to debit a large account, or that one of our big clients had made a mistake in billing. After some thorough checking, it soon became apparent that we had no answers for this appalling lack of funds. Then, overshadowing that problem, was Mary's sudden disappearance, which has greatly upset all of us."

For the first time on this case, Michael's mental clock was ticking, his instincts were in place, and a dozen different scenarios were playing across his mind.

"Mrs. McCreary, is it possible that Mary could have discovered this mistake, and even known who was responsible?"

She hesitated for a moment before nodding, as she looked directly at Michael. "Actually, it was through Mary's records that we traced the mistake."

There was a few moments of thoughtful silence. Then Mrs. McCreary was the first to speak. "I don't mean to imply anything against Mary, but I tend to agree with your theory. To me, it's always made more sense that her disappearance might have been planned by someone who knew she was on to them."

"Someone here in the office?"

Mrs. McCreary's eyes swept over their heads to the glass wall through which she studied the employees working diligently at their desks. "I find it difficult to believe that anyone here would do such a thing," she answered slowly. "But then, you never know what goes on with employees once they leave this building. I'll give you two or three names. We have one employee whose son is heavily involved in drugs, another woman did not opt for our insurance and has very poor coverage. Now her daughter needs a kidney transplant, and she's trying to raise thirty thousand dollars. Then, one young lady has been with us for only six months."

She began to scribble names on a yellow legal pad. "I'll give you their home addresses and telephone numbers," she said, reaching for her Rolodex, "and I would appreciate it if you conducted a quiet investigation where these people are concerned. Two of them in particular would be insulted if they thought —"

"I understand," Michael said, waiting quietly as Mrs. McCreary flipped through the Rolodex and wrote down addresses and phone numbers.

As she did this, Michael's eyes slipped across to Elizabeth, whose face reflected her surprise over the news they had just heard.

"Here you are," Mrs. McCreary said, carefully tearing out the sheet of names, folding the page neatly, and handing it to Michael.

"I appreciate this," Michael said, placing the paper in the pocket of his shirt. "I promise to be very discreet." He hesitated. "Wyn never mentioned this discrepancy to me. Can you explain why he might not have done that?"

She was thoughtful for a minute. "Well, he knew about it, of course, but he just never felt that Mary had any useful information or she would have come to him first. Naturally he's concerned and wants to keep abreast of what's being done, but for now his primary interest is in locating his fiancée."

"Of course," Elizabeth said, smiling at Mrs. McCreary, then glancing at Michael. "Well, we should let you get back to work. Thank you so much for your time."

"You're more than welcome. It would make me awfully sad to think that someone out there had anything to do with Mary's disappearance," she said, staring again at the people seated behind their desks, efficiently doing their work. "But if that proves to be true, then the person needs to be exposed. The important thing is getting Mary back."

Michael nodded, turning to gaze at the backs of the twenty or so people seated at their desks. "Could you point out to me the people whose names you've given me?"

"Certainly. Virginia Redgrave, the tall, auburn-haired woman in the front row has the son with the drug problem. Sue Wilkens, the gray-haired lady there in the center seat of the second row, has the daughter who needs a transplant. The newest member of our team is the pretty brunette in the end seat of the last row. Her name is Erin Oldham. She's only twenty-six. I find it hard to believe that she could mastermind something like this."

Michael sighed. "You never know. Sometimes wise women make foolish choices in men."

"She isn't married."

"Then a boyfriend may be manipulating her. Believe me, Mrs. McCreary, I've seen it happen before."

The woman closed her eyes and shook her head. "You know, I personally hired each employee out there. If one of them turns out to be a criminal, I'm going to be pretty disappointed in my own judgment."

"Don't blame yourself," Michael said gently. "Sometimes people can be very deceptive. Well, thanks again. And I hope we haven't ruined your day."

"Not at all. If I've given you any information that might help to locate Mary—or our missing money—you will have made my day. You will have made my *year*," she added.

They shook hands again and went back out to meet Claire for lunch.

As soon as they approached Claire's desk, she was reaching for her purse in a bottom drawer. Elizabeth made conversation with her, giving Michael a chance to look at each woman that Mrs. McCreary had indicated. All three faces were intent on their work, as though unaware of the strangers' presence. Michael agreed with Mrs. McCreary that all three women looked like efficient workers. For a split second the young woman, Erin, looked across and locked eyes with Michael. Then she quickly looked back at the screen of her computer.

She was a lovely girl with shining brown hair and blue eyes, medium height, it appeared, and she wore a fashionable dress of navy linen. The dress was well cut, the quality of linen was expensive. Michael wondered how much she earned at this job.

"Ready, Michael?" Elizabeth asked.

He was sizing up the other two women, both middle-aged. The gray-haired lady whose daughter needed a transplant looked tired and intense as she worked. She did not in any way acknowledge their presence. Michael found that a bit strange since her desk was not far from where they stood.

"I'm ready," he said, turning back to Elizabeth.

As they left the office, he cast a glance toward the auburn-haired woman and met a bold, challenging stare. There was no masking her curiosity about him, and he felt another twinge of suspicion.

Michael weighed the options that had been given him as they rode the elevator down to the lobby. While Michael mentally reviewed what Mrs. McCreary had told him, he was grateful to Elizabeth for chatting with Claire, leaving him free to think. Their conversation ran to general topics—workload, hometown, boyfriend. None of Claire's answers came as a surprise. She was overworked, born and raised in Knoxville, and, yes, she had a boyfriend.

When they had reached the impressive lobby, the three of them stopped at the registration desk to sign out. Again Michael met the outright stare of the woman behind the desk. She would be a good one to interview, he decided, for it was doubtful that she ever missed anyone's coming or going, or their reason for doing so. He made a mental note to question her later as he pushed the revolving door for Elizabeth and Claire to exit, then followed behind them.

Once they were out on the busy street, he turned to Claire. "Where do you recommend having lunch?"

Claire looked up and down the street. "There's a good Italian restaurant at the end of the block, if you like Italian food."

"Love it," Elizabeth and Michael replied in unison.

It was a pleasant day, where everyone walked around in long sleeves without sweater or jacket, one of those perfect autumn days when the sunlight is softer and yet there is just enough crispness to the air to be invigorating. Shoppers and businesspeople walked along, looking pleasant yet purposeful.

"It's amazing what a difference a nice day can make in people's moods, isn't it?" Michael asked conversationally. He wanted to keep Claire relaxed so she would feel comfortable with them and talk freely about Mary.

"Yes, it is," Claire agreed as they reached the front door of the restaurant.

Michael pushed the door open, and the aroma of flavorful spices enticed customers to sample the food. Most of the restaurant's patrons were the young working crowd, along with a family seated beneath a lace-filigreed window, and a couple of college girls comparing notes over a textbook. The mood was relaxed. Michael breathed a sigh. This was a pleasant change from the formality of the Dalton corporate offices, and even a nice contrast to their mountain setting.

The hostess led the way back to an empty booth in a far corner. The terra-cotta walls provided a nice background for World War II posters, Elvis memorabilia, and lush tropical plants. Overhead, ceiling fans whirled slowly, keeping a lazy rhythm to the love song flowing from stereo speakers.

They were seated in deep booths, with Michael and Elizabeth facing Claire.

"Look at that." Michael nodded toward a cook flipping a pizza crust. Elizabeth glanced through the opening to the kitchen and smiled.

"I like their tables," Claire said, tracing a fingernail over the laminated top. Beneath it, travel postcards, baseball cards, and ticket stubs were attractively grouped.

"I like this too." Elizabeth smiled at Claire. "What do you recommend for lunch?"

"That's a tough question," she said as they opened the menus.

After a few minutes of mulling over the choices, they decided to share a large pizza, deep dish with the works. A pitcher of iced tea was placed on their table along with tall frosted glasses.

After their server dashed off with their order, Michael came right to the point.

"Claire, since you worked next to Mary, you may be able to help us."

Her eyes grew serious. "I hope so."

"You get to know a person pretty well when you work beside her day after day for—how long?"

Claire looked thoughtful. "I've been at Dalton for two years. I came from a smaller architectural office down the street. I heard of an opening in accounting and went to Dalton's corporate office for an interview. I was delighted when I got the job. The benefits and salary exceed most other businesses. But back to Mary," she said quickly, as though realizing she had strayed from Michael's question. "She came to work at Dalton right after I did."

"Tell us your opinion of Mary," Elizabeth said. "And you can feel free to say whatever you want. It will go no further."

She smiled. "Oh, I have nothing but good things to say about Mary, so I wouldn't mind anyone knowing that. She was always helpful and willing to pitch in if there was an overload." She looked toward a high window, covered in more filigree. "In some ways I think I may have been Mary's closest friend. We had a lot in common. We both came from meager backgrounds—my parents own a small dry-cleaning business in west Knoxville, but with six children in the family, we had to live very conservatively. Mary, of course, lived with her father until he died. He had a good job here at Dalton in the Maintenance Department. In fact, he was head of Maintenance."

"What was her father like?" Elizabeth asked, wanting to know everything about Mary.

"He was pleasant, like Mary, but very quiet. The kind of man who does his job well and minds his own business and doesn't seem to be interested in anyone else's business. He was well liked. The Daltons certainly liked him. He was a devoted employee. Mary said he had always worked for the Daltons.

You probably know Mary's mother died when Mary was sixteen. So she and her dad were very close. He died suddenly of a heart attack after Mary came to work here. Losing her dad was very difficult for her. The Daltons have been a family to Mary."

"I see." Michael nodded. "I believe Wyn said his parents paid her way through business school."

Claire nodded. "That's right. Mary's mother was injured in an auto accident and later died as a result of those injuries." Claire sighed. "Unfortunately Mrs. Chamblis ran a red light and hit another car. The driver of the car sued the Chamblises for damages. Between the lawsuit and the series of operations that Mrs. Chamblis required after the wreck, they were financially drained. She did not work outside the home, so there was only Mr. Chamblis's income for the support of three people."

A huge pizza was spread before them, and for a moment all three stared at the variety of toppings and extra cheese spread over the thick brown crust.

"Well, let's dig in," Michael said as the server gave each of them a plate.

Claire spread a red linen napkin over her lap and reached for a slice of pizza. "Mary told me once that what she really wanted to do was go to art school, but her father felt the most logical choice was learning a trade, which she could do in two years. She was good with computer work and quick with figures. The Daltons knew that, of course, and offered to send her to business school. Naturally they wanted her to come to work for their company when she finished her training. And she did."

Michael chewed his food, thinking about what Claire had said. "Did she like her work?"

Claire hesitated. "She was very thorough and tried to do her work perfectly. Mary was so eager to please," she said, looking sad. "She really appreciated what the Daltons had done for them—first medical bills for her parents, then her tuition and her job. But she once told me that she still longed to do something more creative. Like her mother, she enjoyed sewing. She made curtains for her bathroom and kitchen. I suggested to her that after she married Wyn, she could have a nice home and put all of her creative energy to work there. She liked that idea."

"About Wyn," Michael said, feeling as though they had missed a vital point in the story. "Did they meet when she came to work here?"

"No. They had known each other growing up. The Daltons entertained often, and Mr. Chamblis was a great cook. He often did their barbecuing at large gatherings, and Mary came along to help out." For the first time, a smile touched Claire's lips. "She's a very pretty girl, with beautiful blond hair and a nice figure. After she could afford to dress well, she looked absolutely wonderful. She turned many heads, I can tell you," Claire laughed.

"So she obviously turned Wyn's head," Elizabeth said, smiling.

"I think Wyn has always been in love with her," Claire sighed.

"How did the Daltons feel about that?" Michael asked curiously.

A tiny frown hovered between her brown brows for a brief moment. "Mary said that in the beginning they wanted a social type for him, but he had gone out with many of those. Mary had a bit of a mystique about her, and I think that fascinated Wyn."

"A mystique?" Michael repeated, reaching for another slice of pizza.

"Yes. Well, let me put it this way. It's as though you know someone and yet you sense the person may be holding something back. Mary was like that. She and I had some very serious conversations, but then she would stop short of a real confidence." She looked at Elizabeth. "You know how girls become close friends and confide in one another. I would spill my guts to her," she laughed, "and she would always listen carefully, maybe even give me some wise advice, and yet she was a private person. Although I sometimes wanted to ask her questions about Wyn and their relationship, I found myself stopping short of prying. I felt she would volunteer what she wanted me to know."

Michael and Elizabeth stared at her for a moment. Then Michael spoke up again. "Was she in love with Wyn?"

Claire seemed taken aback by the question. She blinked, as though wondering if she had heard correctly. "Of course she was! She was always saying she didn't know what Wyn saw in her, but, of course, it was apparent when he stopped at her desk each day or when they left together. He looked at her with absolute adoration. She was a very sweet person, a bit shy, almost passive, I guess I could say. Or at least she was with Wyn."

Claire paused for a moment, taking a long sip of her tea. "One thing you've probably noticed is that Wyn likes to be in control, to be the boss. Mary suited him because she was not the liberal, independent type. She seemed to want someone she could rely on. I think her parents' deaths affected her greatly."

They had managed to demolish most of the pizza. As the conversation wound down, Michael wondered what other information he could obtain from Claire, even though she had already told them a lot.

"So you think Mary was excited about the wedding? Looking forward to being Wyn's wife?"

Claire laughed. "She was pretty nervous about it. She didn't want a big wedding, but the Daltons felt that because of their wide social circle, there should be a large number of guests. I know Mary was giving a lot of thought to that. She would bring brides' magazines to work with her, and she had a book of etiquette that she pored over at every opportunity."

"Well," Elizabeth sighed, shaking her head, "it sounds to me as though she was a girl who had everything, or was about to have everything. That makes this seem even more tragic."

"Claire," Michael said, lowering his voice, "what is your theory of all this? Can you see a motive for someone's abducting her?"

Claire hesitated, taking a deep breath. "Well, as Mrs. McCreary has already told you, our department was unable to balance the books this past month. There was a huge mistake somewhere. I think Mary really worried about that. Being so close to the Daltons, it was like she felt it her personal responsibility to try to figure out what happened."

"Is it possible an employee at Dalton abducted her?" Michael asked, point blank.

"You know, that makes more sense to me than anything else," Claire said in a low voice. "I wouldn't begin to venture a guess as to who that might have been, or how she was grabbed from right under Wyn's nose, but she was obviously troubled during her last week of work. I could see that she was trying to figure something out; she even worked through a couple of lunch hours, going over her records."

"Do you think she ever figured out what was wrong?"

Claire pursed her lips. "I honestly can't say. She quit going out for lunch that week, said she had no appetite. And she was a thin girl anyway. I told her if she didn't start eating, she would have to have her wedding gown altered. She said she tried to eat but she just didn't have any appetite."

"What about her last day of work? The Friday before she and Wyn went up to the mountains?"

Claire nodded. "She was very quiet and thoughtful. I remember her asking if I had any aspirin. She looked as though she didn't feel well. But she never told me what was bothering her. Perhaps she confided in Wyn."

"I'll ask him. From all indications, their date was just a pleasant Saturday drive to the mountains."

Claire nodded. "Mary loved the mountains. She said she always felt a sense of peace when she could spend some time there. She loved shopping in the little stores and just hanging out there in general. I imagine it was exactly what she needed after that hard week."

Michael had one more question, which he tried to phrase as delicately as possible. "Claire, you seem to be a very perceptive woman. So I want to ask you something else. This may seem like an odd question, but believe me, it's routine. After Mary disappeared, what was your impression of Wyn's reaction to her disappearance?"

Claire's head jerked up, obviously startled by the question. "Oh, he was devastated. He stayed up there for a few days, working with the sheriff, but he kept someone at his condo to check the phone calls in case there was a ransom call. Then, fearing his place was being watched, he came home and never left for the next two days. There was still no ransom call."

She sighed as her eyes drifted into space. "After a week or so, he came back to work, but he was obviously preoccupied. He was short tempered, nervous, anxious, jumping at every phone call. The secretary up in his office was ready to quit, I think. Then Wyn saw a doctor and got something for his nerves. After that, he was better. Or maybe that was about the time he hired you to try to locate Mary. I think you've given him some hope."

Michael frowned. "I know. He seems to have placed a lot of faith in my finding her. I have to tell you, this is a very difficult case."

They went back to the remnants of their food, with everyone deep in thought for the next few minutes until Michael spoke again. "The most obvious possibility of what may have happened to her leads back to your department, Claire. What can you tell me about the people in that department?"

Claire stopped eating. "I was afraid you were going to ask me that."

"Why were you afraid?" Elizabeth asked gently.

"Because…well…because I don't want to falsely accuse anyone or cast doubt in the wrong direction." She hesitated, started to speak, then pushed her plate away.

"Okay, so let me put your mind at ease," Michael said smoothly. "We're just speculating here. We aren't accusing anyone of anything. But if you were in my shoes, as the detective, would you check out Mrs. Redgrave, Mrs. Wilkens, or the new girl—what's her name?" He snapped his fingers as though trying to remember.

"Erin Oldham." Her eyes grew sad as she looked from Michael to Elizabeth. "I guess I would check all of them out. But I would probably search deeper into the lifestyle of the new girl, specifically her boyfriend."

Michael nodded thoughtfully. "Do you have any idea why Wyn didn't suggest this to me?"

She shook her head. "No. Probably because he trusts Mrs. McCreary so much in selecting and overseeing employees.

She's been with them for a very long time. And I think he's convinced that whoever took Mary was someone far more sinister than an employee of his company." She shrugged. "I heard he still believes there's a possibility that she fell off that mountaintop and the searchers have failed to locate her. He hasn't exactly made a secret of the fact that he's not impressed with the sheriff and his staff."

Michael nodded. "And yet it's their jurisdiction."

Elizabeth touched Michael's hand. "That's why Wyn was so thrilled when you called. He said he had already hired one private investigator but he hadn't turned up anything."

Michael rolled his eyes. "I hate to have so much confidence riding on me if I'm unable to solve this crazy thing."

"You'll solve it," Elizabeth replied confidently.

The server came to refill their drinks, and Michael looked across at Claire. "Okay, let's get back to the three employees we've just discussed. What do you know about Erin Oldham's boyfriend?"

Claire shook her head. "Nothing. That's just it. If you'll notice, she's wearing a diamond dinner ring that's well over a carat. I don't think she bought it for herself on our salary. And no one has met her mysterious boyfriend. She never discusses him."

"How would we find out?" Michael asked.

Claire shrugged. "I suppose you could ask her. She seemed sincerely upset about Mary's disappearance. As for her having other friends, she more or less stays to herself." She glanced at her watch. "It's almost one. I suppose I should be getting back."

Elizabeth looked at Michael. "By all means. We don't want to detain you. It's been very nice talking with you. Thanks for joining us."

"Oh, you're welcome. It was my pleasure." She looked from

Elizabeth to Michael, smiling at both.

Michael stood, handing Claire his business card. "We're staying at the chalet I've indicated on the card. But tonight—" he glanced down at Elizabeth—"what do you think of staying here in Knoxville tonight, Elizabeth?"

"That's fine with me."

"There's a nice hotel over on the next block," Claire said and gave them the name and address. "I don't think you would have any problem getting a room there on a weeknight. On weekends during football season at UT, they're always booked."

Michael nodded. "Then we'll be staying there tonight if you think of anything that might be helpful. It may be that our search needs to be localized in this area. We'll see."

"I wish you luck," she said, looking from Michael to Elizabeth. "I would do anything to help Mary. She's one of the nicest people I've ever known."

Michael nodded, and Elizabeth looked sad as they watched Claire leave the restaurant.

EIGHT

Elizabeth cast an apprehensive glance at Michael as he unlocked the door to Mary's condo. She realized that Michael was accustomed to going into someone's private world, taking a look around, making an assessment of that person's tastes and lifestyle. But this was new to her, and she felt anxious and on edge.

The key turned easily in the lock, and Michael opened the door. He glanced at her. "Coming?"

She hesitated. "I feel as though...well, as though we're invading someone's privacy, Michael."

"Honey, Wyn gave us the key," he reminded her. "We aren't breaking and entering. We're going in to seek evidence that may help us to locate Mary Chamblis. Don't you think Mary would appreciate some help?"

Elizabeth sighed. "Of course. I'm just being silly."

They entered the foyer of an ultramodern condo reflecting the taste of someone who enjoyed all of today's modern conveniences. The walls were the color of rich cream, the carpet was white, thick and lush, and the furnishings were the latest in modern design. Abstract art lined the walls, along with one or two very expensive paintings. Everything was neat and in order. Mary had left her condo immaculate that fateful Saturday. And she had not returned. As they wandered through the spacious condo, Elizabeth studied the decorative vases and the massive displays of silk flowers. "She was definitely more like Wyn than we realized."

"What do you mean?"

She shrugged. "I'm not sure. I would have expected a more—I don't know—a more homey touch, for lack of a better way to say it. Everything is chic and upscale for a woman who came from a moderate background."

When they entered Mary's bedroom, Elizabeth noticed a subtle change.

"Now this looks more livable," she said with a nod of approval.

The walls were done in a rich peach color with white trim on the windows and door facings. The queen-size canopy bed had white organdy draped over the canopy and extending down in lush bows on the bedposts. The white eyelet throw pillows held tiny pearls in the shape of an M.

Elizabeth walked over to touch a pillow. "I like this room," she said, glancing around. "It breaks the austerity of the rest of the condo."

"Austerity? That *austerity,* as you put it, cost a lot of money, hon."

"Well, it doesn't quite suit my taste. This does. It's more..." she searched for the right word as she stood in the center of the room, looking around.

"It's more personal," Michael finished for her, and she nodded.

He walked over to the bedside table to lift an eight-by-ten picture frame molded in an expensive gold-leaf design.

It was a portrait of Mary and Wyn, done in a studio. Mary's hair was very short, and its blond color was closer to platinum. Her face was not as thin as the picture now on the flyers, yet it was apparent that she was model thin. Pale brown brows were perfectly arched above brown eyes. She had a slim nose over thin lips covered in an apricot lipstick. The lipstick matched the blush on her high cheekbones, compensating for the hollow cheeks.

Wyn wore a navy blazer, pale blue shirt, and a tie that looked as though it had been designed by someone famous. He looked very much the same as he had in the restaurant, and his smile, like Mary's, was a bit reserved.

"Elizabeth, what's wrong with this picture?" Michael asked, studying it thoughtfully.

Elizabeth wandered over, took a look, and shrugged. "Well, you know me. I like the natural look, but Mary's taste obviously ran to more dramatic coloring."

"No, it's something else. Posed. They look very posed."

"Well, who doesn't in this kind of picture? That's why I prefer to enlarge our snapshots and frame them. But, then again, I'm the natural type."

Michael was still studying the picture, his eyes thoughtful. "I think Wyn and Mary have more in common than we've figured. She's a woman who would turn heads—not mine, of course. It so happens I prefer this natural look you keep mentioning. Mary is obviously very striking, and I think this would appeal to Wyn."

Elizabeth looked at him curiously. "Why do you say that?"

He replaced the picture. "Well, let's face it. Wyn is a regular-looking guy, and I think he would be attracted to someone he could flaunt on his arm at various social functions."

She nodded. "You're right. In my professional experience, that's usually the pattern....Look at this."

She had wandered to the bureau and picked up a picture of a couple that must have been taken in the sixties, judging from the hairstyles and clothing. The couple's faces were wreathed in wide smiles and the unmistakable look of love glowed in their eyes. The woman had dark hair and eyes and wore a pretty red dress; the man had light brown hair, blue eyes, and was quite handsome in his sport coat and tie.

"These must have been Mary's parents," Michael said, staring at the picture. There was something about their expressions, the smiles, the look in their eyes that seemed oddly familiar. What was it?

Elizabeth peered around his shoulder at the picture, then glanced up at her husband. "Michael, they look happier than Wyn and Mary."

"I would guess it's because they lived a simple life and didn't require a lot to be happy. Like my folks. Remember Mary's mother stayed at home and was wife and mother—"

"That was back in the days when women had little training for outside jobs." She was always quick to defend women's professions because she believed that the modern world required two incomes and a woman comfortable with her own status.

"I know, darling. And I'm not casting any aspersions on today's woman. I'm just saying these people look more content than Wyn and Mary."

As Elizabeth glanced across the room at the other picture, she had to agree. "Yeah, I wish my father hadn't been killed in Vietnam," she said wistfully.

He took her into his arms. "So do I. I'd like to have known him."

For a moment her eyes filled with tears, but then she blinked them away and kissed him. "I'm just glad that Katie and I have you."

"And we're glad we have you. Now back to our search."

They spent the next hour going through closets and drawers, looking for any kind of information that might shed some light on Mary's life. They found nothing of importance. Her wardrobe reflected that of a fashionable working woman, with everything neatly in place. Even the shoes were lined up side by side on little white racks, with matching handbags in another rack.

"She obviously hasn't been here, nor has anyone else," Michael finally concluded. "And there's nothing out of place to indicate that someone was snooping around for something."

They walked into the kitchen and opened the refrigerator. There was nothing inside.

Elizabeth looked at him. "That's strange."

"She may have a maid who comes in and cleans stuff out, but I'll ask Wyn."

As they opened the cabinets, they found boxes of herbal tea and various sacks of flour, sugar, and cornmeal, along with a lazy Susan full of spices. Only a few canned goods lined the shelves, the variety that would keep indefinitely. It was obvious no one had lived here in a while.

"I imagine they ate out a lot," Elizabeth concluded.

Michael nodded as he thrust his hands on his hips and looked around the room. "Well, I guess we're back to square one."

"So what do we do now?"

"Now we start investigating those three people in her office. They're looking more suspicious to me all the time. If someone worked with her, knew her habits, and overheard that she and Wyn were going to drive up to the mountains, they could have followed. When Wyn went into the restroom, it was the perfect opportunity for that person to drive up, grab Mary, and be gone before Wyn came out."

"And if he heard a vehicle leaving, he would have assumed it was the van."

"Right."

They looked at each other, their excitement mounting.

"Where do we begin?" Elizabeth asked eagerly.

Michael opened his notebook, checking the names again. "Let's start with the most recent employee, the young lady

Claire feels most inclined to suspect. Erin Oldham."

He glanced at his watch. "It's after four now. What do you say we scope out her place to see if there's a live-in boyfriend coming or going?"

"Sounds like a good plan."

"While I have a phone at my disposal, I'm going to make a reservation at the hotel Claire suggested, then call Wyn and tell him where we'll be. I also want to ask him more about these employees."

First Michael made a reservation at the hotel; then he called Wyn, who was out. He left a telephone number with Wyn's secretary where he and Elizabeth could be reached that evening. Then he replaced the white telephone in its cradle and reached for Elizabeth's hand.

"Let's get out of here. Something about this place depresses me."

"Me too," Elizabeth said, frowning. They slipped out of the quiet condominium and locked the door. The red carpeted hallway made only a light whisper beneath their footsteps as they walked back to the elevator. Elizabeth kept thinking about Mary Chamblis, wondering where she was now. And if she was alive.

Elizabeth looked across the darkened front seat of the car and shook her head at Michael.

"I never knew a stakeout could be so boring," she said on a yawn.

They were parked just down the street from Erin Oldham's garden home, watching her driveway, which was empty.

"At least you're getting to see what my job is all about," Michael responded.

"In the *beginning*, this was what your job was all about. That's why Katie and I saw so little of you. And I do understand that now. I'm just grateful you can afford to hire someone else to do this kind of stakeout when you're in Atlanta. Speaking of which, on the salary Wyn is paying you, couldn't we just hire someone to spy on Erin?"

"We could, but then we'd miss out on the fun. Come on, love. It takes patience to be a good detective."

Elizabeth glanced at the clock on the dash of the car. "It's six o'clock, and Dalton Chemicals closed at five. Where is she?"

As soon as the words were out of her mouth, car lights flashed around the end of the block, and a white Nissan slowed down and wheeled into the driveway.

"Bingo!" Michael said as Elizabeth bolted upright in her seat.

They watched Erin get out of her car, open the back door and reach in for a sack. As she closed the door, Michael looked through his binoculars. "Winn Dixie is stamped on the side of the sack."

"So our mystery gal is not so mysterious, after all. She goes to the grocery just like I do."

"Shhh."

"Why are you shushing me? She can't hear us."

"I need to concentrate," Michael answered absently as they watched Erin shift the groceries and fumble with her keys.

Soon the front door was unlocked, an inside foyer light went on, and the door closed.

"Michael, please don't tell me we're going to sit here all night just staring at her house. She came home alone, and there's no one else in that dark house, and no other car in the driveway."

"No, we won't sit here all night, I promise. But I spotted the top of a wine bottle jutting out of that sack. Let's just wait and see if she's expecting company."

"And if nobody comes, let's go inside and find out what she's having for dinner. I'm starving, aren't you?"

He pulled down the binoculars and frowned across at her. "I told you, Elizabeth, you have to be patient. You'll soon have me wondering if I should have left you back at the chalet."

"No, you shouldn't have left me," she quickly added, thinking about how cute Erin was, with a figure that looked perfect. "But I do trust you," she added, more to herself than to Michael.

"This is a weeknight. Why would she be buying a bottle of wine on a weeknight?"

"Maybe she just likes wine."

Lights spilled from windows onto the side yard, then the light was slatted as though blinds had just been closed.

"The bedroom. She'll change clothes now." Michael looked at Elizabeth. "I'll make you a bet that she'll be having company soon."

"You're on," Elizabeth said, still sure that Erin was just getting dinner and snacks for a night of watching television. "How long do we have to wait?"

Michael sighed. "Why don't I just call a cab for you?"

"No," she argued stubbornly, "I can be as patient as you."

She laid her head against the back of the seat and tried not to think about how good a hamburger and French fries would taste. They had passed a fast-food restaurant on the next block, and she could almost smell the French fries now as her stomach growled. She swallowed hard, determined not to complain.

Their wait turned out to be brief. Twenty minutes later the front door opened, and Erin bounded out dressed in a workout suit. The lime color of the suit was practically fluorescent beneath her porch light.

Elizabeth's mouth dropped open. She had the kind of figure women dreamed about. Curves and hollows in the right places, long legs and a pretty face framed with gleaming brown hair. If there was any doubt about her perfect figure, the low-cut cropped top and matching tights dispelled those doubts. An expensive brand of tennis shoes completed the stunning outfit.

"See, she isn't staying home after all," Michael said.

"She's going to a gym. Big deal."

"Kind of a contradiction, don't you think? Coming in with wine and goodies and then taking off to the gym. Let's follow her." He started the car.

"Can we zip through and get a hamburger along the way?" Elizabeth asked hopefully.

"Not until we see where she's going," Michael replied matter-of-factly.

Elizabeth took a deep breath and bit her lip. She had begged to come along on this investigation; the least she could do was keep her mouth shut and not bug Michael when he was trying to do his job.

"She's not messing around," he said, accelerating the Blazer so that they could keep up with her.

Elizabeth cast a wistful eye toward the fast-food restaurant as they breezed past. She wished she'd had the presence of mind to at least pick up some fruit earlier.

Michael kept his distance as Erin zipped down one street then another and finally pulled into the parking lot of a swanky-looking gym. The parking lot was filled with a number of expensive vehicles, with only a few suggesting middle-class incomes.

"Hmm," Michael said, parking at a safe distance. "This could be interesting. I'd say a membership here would require a hefty chunk out of her salary. Wonder why she chose this particular gym rather than a more modest one? The equipment can't be that much better."

"This one probably has one of those fancy juice bars, tanning beds, an Olympic-sized, indoor pool, all the little things to pamper a girl." Suddenly Elizabeth perked up. "Want me to go in and snoop around? She might remember us if we go in together, but I'll put my hair up and keep my back turned, so she won't notice me."

"How exactly do you plan to spy on her? Join her on the jogging track?"

Elizabeth was twisting her hair around her fingers, pressing it to the back of her head, and inserting a white hair clip she had left in the glove compartment. "I'll go in and inquire about a membership," she told Michael smugly. "If they offer a tour of the facilities, I'll say I prefer to look around on my own. Why won't that work?"

He shrugged. "Go for it."

She hopped out of the car, feeling her adrenaline soar. At last she was getting in on the action, and it felt good. Erin had already disappeared behind the huge double doors. Elizabeth lagged for a moment, giving Erin time to choose her preference in exercise equipment.

Then, satisfied she had waited long enough, Elizabeth lifted her chin confidently and opened the door. She came face-to-face with a buxom blond behind an oval reception desk. The receptionist had to be a college girl moonlighting, Elizabeth decided, from the dewy look of youth on her face. Or there really was a carrot-juice bar here.

"Hi," Elizabeth called, glancing toward the huge glass enclosure that housed all varieties of exercise equipment. Both men and women were lifting, straining, and sweating, but there was no sign of Erin.

"Do you have your card?" the girl asked politely. "Sorry, but I forget faces. There are so many people coming and going that it's hard to remember everyone. And I only work the three-to-eleven shift."

"That's okay." Elizabeth gave her a charming smile. "Actually, I'm thinking of joining, and I just wanted to look around."

"Oh." The girl perked up. No doubt she worked on commission as well as salary. "I'll page Tommy to come give you a tour of—"

"If you don't mind, I'd prefer to wander around on my own. Then I might ask Tommy to give me some instructions on the weights."

The girl's eyes swept down Elizabeth's slim figure. "Sure. I'll be happy to answer any questions you might have. If I don't know, Tommy will."

Will he? Elizabeth thought, her eyes sweeping around in search of Erin.

"Do you want an aerobics schedule?"

"Not just yet."

"What about membership fees?" the girl asked, testing Elizabeth's interest.

Elizabeth shrugged and gave her a little smile. "That won't be a problem."

"Oh." The girl's smile widened and she began to point out the various areas—the jogging track, handball court, and swimming pool were on the basement level. "Some of the exercise equipment is in there," she said, indicating the area Elizabeth had already spotted. "And the treadmills are down that hallway," she said, pointing. "We also have a prenatal gym, as well as a nursery, if you're interested," she added, noting the wedding ring on Elizabeth's finger. "The locker rooms, sauna, and Jacuzzi are that way." She pointed in the opposite direction. "Along with the aerobics department."

"Sounds perfect," Elizabeth said, folding her hands behind her back. "I'll just wander around."

Since Erin had already disappeared when Elizabeth walked through the door, she ruled out the long hallway leading toward the locker rooms and aerobics. She opted instead to check out the shorter hallway leading to the treadmills. Heading in that direction, she spotted Erin right away...being real cozy with the guy on the treadmill adjoining hers. From a discreet distance, Elizabeth watched them, noting the way their eyes locked onto each other's, the way they moved their mouths in private conversation. A happy bubble of laughter tumbled from Erin's curving mouth, and the man stared at her lips.

He was at least forty years old, with a nice physique, dark hair, and a handsome square face. The look he was giving Erin was not healthy. And the response she sent back was warm enough to burn a few calories.

This had to be the boyfriend, only there was something wrong here. The man wore a wedding band on his left hand—and Erin was not married.

Elizabeth took a slow, thorough look at the other treadmills—at least ten—where four other women and three men moved at various speeds. None of them seemed to be as delighted with their workout as Erin and her friend. Furthermore, there were three treadmills not in use, so there was no mistaking the fact that Erin had deliberately chosen this treadmill, or that the man had been here for a while. His jogging shorts and T-shirt bore the slight stain of perspiration.

Elizabeth scooted back around the corner, then came to a dead halt before the reception desk. The girl was engaged in a telephone conversation, detailing the merits of belonging to the gym. She motioned to Elizabeth that she would be right with her. Elizabeth lifted her hand and wiggled her fingers in a cute little wave. "Be back." She moved her lips slowly with emphasis so as not to interrupt the girl's conversation.

Then she was out the door before the girl could hang up the phone.

When she reported to Michael what she had observed, he looked astonished. "It always disappoints me when a pretty young woman like Erin Oldham is attracted to an older married man. And yet it happens more frequently than we know about, I imagine."

"So what do we do now?" she asked, energized by their game.

"We wait."

When she groaned, Michael reached across the car seat and squeezed her hand. "I have a feeling she won't be in there much longer."

Michael was right. In less than thirty minutes, Erin came bouncing out, looking more rejuvenated than ever. She unlocked her car, hopped in, and started the engine.

"Now, let's see where she goes," Michael said, giving her time to get to the edge of the parking lot before he started the Blazer.

"She's going back home," Elizabeth said, somewhat amazed, as they retraced the route back down the same streets, ending up at her garden home.

This time, however, she parked in front rather than in the driveway. She was out of the car and in the house in record time. More lights flashed across the yard. In less than five minutes a white Mercedes turned down the block, driving slowly. The car passed Erin's driveway, then stopped and backed carefully into the garage. The garage door went down.

"He thinks he has everyone fooled," Elizabeth sputtered. "Outrageous!"

Michael started the car. "Well, I don't think we'll wait any longer. We know the ending to this little chapter."

"Do you think Mary found out about them and threatened to tell?"

He shook his head. "Doesn't feel right. Of course, we don't know who the guy is, but I have his license number, and it shouldn't be difficult to get his name."

Elizabeth looked across at him, amazed. "How did you read his license so quickly? He backed up before I even got a glimpse."

"I got it in the parking lot while you were nosing around inside." He took his notebook and its attached pen down from the visor. "There's a list of every car, make, model, and license number in the parking lot."

"How did you manage that?" she asked, wide-eyed.

He winked. "I'm quick. Otherwise, I wouldn't be a good detective."

She nodded, and then she found herself thinking of the past, how she had failed to appreciate how hard he worked to try to find people. Too bad his career and hers had led them into different directions. But at least they were back together again. And God had blessed them abundantly with a daughter like Katie.

"I think we need to call Katie," she said suddenly, her thoughts turning toward their daughter as they reached the hotel. "I really miss her."

"So do I." Michael glanced quickly at his watch. "We're too late. She's already in bed. We'll call her first thing in the morning, okay? Incidentally, that makes me think of Jay. I left word for him to call me tonight about his trip to Birmingham. He'll call the chalet since he doesn't know we're staying in Knoxville."

Once they were inside their hotel room, Michael reached for the phone and began to punch in his credit-card number. "Maybe we'll get a break on the other end," he said, cradling the phone against his shoulder as he looked back at Elizabeth, who was snuggling under the covers.

"Hello," Jay answered wearily.

"Hey, brother, you sound tired."

"Well, it's not every day I travel to Birmingham and back, not to mention the time spent questioning those people. I don't think they had anything to do with it, Michael."

"You don't?" Michael leaned back against the pillows, gripping the phone. "Neither does Sheriff Grayson. I guess I was just hoping you'd turn up something he missed."

"Before I went up there, I made some phone calls, looked into their background, all the routine stuff. A speeding ticket was all I could dig up. There's just no motive for their abducting Mary Chamblis. But I don't mind going on with the investigation if you think it's warranted."

Michael sighed. "No, but I'd appreciate it if you'd follow up with the police department in Bessemer just to keep tabs on them."

"I've already planned that. I may be wrong, but all my instincts tell me they're honest."

"And I trust your instincts. Thanks, Jay. We'll treat you guys to dinner when we get back."

"We'll look forward to it. Good luck, Michael."

"Thanks. But I'm going to need more than luck on this one. It's beginning to look as though we'll need a miracle."

"Well, we both know who the Miracle Worker is."

Michael smiled. "Right. Thanks, Jay."

After he hung up and related the phone conversation to Elizabeth, she nodded solemnly. "He's right. We haven't really prayed about this. I think it's time we started."

They joined hands and spent the next few minutes praying for the safety of Mary Chamblis and asking God for direction in leading them to her.

After their prayer, Michael took a deep breath and realized he could no longer postpone phoning his employer to bring him up to date on the latest news he and Elizabeth had uncovered about the people in the accounting department. Specifically Erin and the mysterious boyfriend who happened to be married.

To Michael's surprise, Wyn was not thrilled with this bit of news when Michael related what he had discovered about Erin. Wyn made no response when he was informed of the clandestine meeting, so Michael plunged on, giving a description of the man and promising to have his name by morning.

The sigh that came over the telephone wires from Wyn was deep and heavy. "Michael, don't waste your time. I know the man. I belong to the same gym. And believe me, there's no reason for them to kidnap Mary. Is that where you've been all this time?" A note of sarcasm now underlined his tone.

Michael bristled. "That's not the only place, no." He related the conversation he had with Mrs. McCreary. "You didn't mention the missing funds. To me, we've uncovered the first motive of any substance. I'd be a fool not to follow these leads."

There was a pause. "Sorry. You're right, of course. I just have trouble believing that one of our employees would kidnap Mary."

"What about the woman whose health insurance doesn't cover a kidney transplant? Sue Wilkens."

There was a pause. "I know the girl has to have the transplant, but we have a fund going at the office. I can't believe Sue would…" his voice trailed.

"Wyn, this is a strange case. I think we're going to have to check out every possibility. What about Virginia Redgrave? Her son has a drug problem."

"Yeah, that would be the most likely guess, if I had to make one. I thought he was in a rehab clinic someplace."

"How can you find out?"

"I'll simply phone her. Tell her someone approached me today wanting the name of a good clinic. She may or may not believe it, doesn't matter. I want to know where this guy is. She's always had problems with him. The dad took off when he was a kid."

"Okay, I'll be waiting for your call," Michael said, hanging up. He looked at Elizabeth. "He just doesn't want to believe they could have erred so badly in judgment and installed someone with sticky fingers to handle their money."

"So does he think Virginia has sticky fingers?"

"You always have to look at the motive, hon. Both women have motives that would tear at your heart and ease your conscience a bit. As a parent, you know it gets easy to be a little selfish where your child is concerned."

Elizabeth nodded sadly.

Michael picked up the phone again, checking his notebook's pocket for numbers. In a few minutes he was dialing again, and Elizabeth looked at him and thought how grateful she was that he could handle situations so well. She didn't know how. The possibility of a mother's being pushed to desperation for her child troubled her.

"Hi, Ben, this is Michael," he was saying. "Heard any news on Mary Chamblis? Okay. Well, thanks for checking. See you soon."

Elizabeth leaned forward, hoping somehow a miracle would intervene and ease everyone's mind.

Michael merely shook his head as he hung up the phone. "Ben's going to Cherokee tomorrow. Maybe he'll hear something. Will you catch the phone if Wyn calls back?"

"Sure." She reached for the remote to turn off the boring comedy she had been trying to watch. Her thoughts were filled with Sue Wilkens and Virginia Redgrave. Which one had the strongest motive? Or the fewest scruples?

Michael was singing in the shower when the telephone rang. Elizabeth grabbed it on the second ring.

"Elizabeth? This is Wyn."

"Hi, Wyn."

"I spoke with Virginia. She claims that Charlie is in a hospital in Nashville. She even gave me the telephone number."

Elizabeth frowned. "Then he must be there."

"Ask Michael to find out for me. Will you be coming by the office in the morning?"

"I imagine we will be. Are you tied up?"

"If you can get there before ten, I can cancel my first appointment. After that, I have an appointment that I absolutely cannot cancel."

"We'll be there shortly after eight," she said, glancing at the clock.

The water had been turned off in the shower, and now she could hear Michael brushing his teeth and gargling.

Two suspects down and one to go, she thought. She really hated to think about a mother whose daughter would die without a kidney transplant, a mother who could possibly be the villain in this mystery.

NINE

B en walked out of the bookstore in Cherokee, pleased with the history book he had just acquired to add to his collection. The material for his thesis was stacking up, box after box, until he would soon be out of space in his room at the boardinghouse.

Early-morning shoppers milled along the sidewalk, and he was just turning toward the coffee shop when he spotted Raven. She was wearing a white cotton dress with a beaded bodice, and if it was possible, she was more beautiful than before. Her dark hair and eyes were set off to perfection by the pristine white of her clothing, and her braids were secured with white leather thongs.

He froze in his steps as their eyes met.

"Hello," he called, propelling himself forward.

"Hello," she answered softly.

As he reached her side, he realized, to his good fortune, that they were standing directly in front of the coffee shop where a small patio out front offered an empty table with two chairs. Perfect, he decided, ready to take the initiative.

"Are you on your way to work?" he asked politely.

She nodded. "Yes. And you?"

"Just about to get a cup of coffee and take a look at a book I just purchased about your people," he said, lifting the sack captioned with the name of the bookstore. "Could you join me for a minute? I wanted to ask you something about the Cherokees. I'm working hard on my thesis," he added.

She turned and glanced at the patio, then back at him. "I don't have long."

"Won't take long for a cup of coffee. And I promise not to detain you," he added, keeping his voice light and pleasant.

She glanced at a couple of businessmen seated at tables, reading newspapers. Then she took a breath and nodded at Ben. "Okay, I'll stop for a minute. But I'll have their special herb tea instead of coffee."

"Great." He pressed his package into her hand. "Want to hold our table while I get the drinks? Check out the book, and see what you think." He bounded off before she could change her mind.

When he returned, she had removed the book from its sack and was reading the back cover.

"Thank you," she said as he placed her tea before her. "This book looks interesting."

He took a seat opposite her and tried to focus his thoughts on conversation. "I'm collecting everything I can find on the subject."

"For your thesis?" she asked, tilting her head to study him as she toyed with her tea bag.

"And for my own collection. I hope to write a book after I graduate."

"You do? About the Cherokee nation?"

He nodded. "And the pioneers and mountain folk. Obviously, I'm fascinated."

She nodded as a faint smile touched her pale lips. "I can see that you are."

He took a sip of coffee and burned his mouth. He tried not to react to that, for he suspected he was behaving like a lovesick schoolboy. He looked into his cup and tried to assemble his thoughts. He considered himself fairly sophisticated; he had acquired many friends in his lifetime, and she certainly wasn't the first girl to turn his head. It was this mountain setting, her dazzling outfit, the novelty of everything, he told himself. But then her soft voice floated across the table to him, bringing his eyes back to her, and his logic evaporated.

"I think it's wonderful that you're trying so hard to be accurate in what you're writing," she was saying. "Many people have tried to write about this land and the people here, but some have turned their material into nothing more than a commercial venture. I'm amazed at the way authors mess up names and dates or don't check their facts closely."

"To be honest," he said, smiling at her, "I enjoy the research more than the writing. I do want to get my facts straight, however. I try to have three sources that agree on the same date or event before I accept it as the truth."

She nodded, studying him over her cup as she delicately sipped her tea. "That's a good idea," she said. Her dark eyes held his for a moment; then she dropped her gaze. She said nothing more, but the silence between them was not uncomfortable. He liked her quiet nature.

He leaned back in the chair, forcing his mind back to the reason he had detained her, for he wanted to talk with her as long as she would stay.

"The last time we spoke, you mentioned you have ancestors who traveled the Trail of Tears," he said.

"Yes, I did," she said gravely. "My great-grandmother was very young in 1838 when the Cherokees were rounded up and taken on the Trail of Tears." Her dark eyes were thoughtful as she paused to stir her tea. "Her parents made a decision at the last minute. They agreed to say good-bye to one another because my great-great-grandfather said he would rather die than have his child raised someplace else. He hid his wife and child in the rocks. He said he would try to escape and come back to them, but he was one of the many who did not survive the long, rugged trip. I'm told he starved to death."

Ben winced and shook his head. "What happened to the wife and child?"

Her eyes drifted back to Ben. "My great-grandmother stayed hidden in a cave with her mother and an aunt, living off wild berries and corn. Eventually they joined a few others who were in hiding as well. My great-grandmother was married at fourteen to a young brave whose parents had also hidden among the rocks. My grandmother was one of their three children. It's a Cherokee tradition that when a woman takes a husband, he becomes part of her family and lives with the wife's family. That's how our line has developed."

Ben nodded, staring at her. "I suspect that somewhere in my lineage there is Cherokee blood, for I've been drawn to this area like a magnet."

She smiled, bringing a sparkle to her dark eyes. "So do you plan to stay on here and write your book?"

"I do, as a matter of fact." Then suddenly he remembered his promise to the Calloways to ask about the missing woman. "By the way, you haven't heard anything more on Mary Chamblis, have you? Michael Calloway called me last night. When I told him I was coming to Cherokee, he wanted me to ask around."

"No, I haven't heard anything." Their eyes locked for a moment, and then she remembered her tea and lifted the cup. "I must go, or I'll be late," she said, draining the cup. "Thank you." She had come to her feet and was leaving before he could pay the bill. He had planned to walk with her to her shop, but she moved away from him with light delicate steps.

He sighed and headed to the counter to pay. As he did, he

cast another glance in her direction. She had already disappeared.

There was fresh coffee and a box of pastries waiting when Elizabeth and Michael arrived in Wyn's office. Again Michael noted the impressive array of diplomas, memberships, and awards. But despite Wyn's money and status, he had been unable to regain the treasure he wanted most, Michael thought as he shook hands with Wyn.

A secretary swept into the room, prepared to serve the coffee and pastries, both of which Wyn declined. "I've already had two cups of coffee. That's my limit. My nerves aren't too good these days, as you can imagine."

After the secretary left, Michael got down to business. "I have some news for you," he said and turned to Wyn. "Mrs. Redgrave's son is not in the Nashville hospital."

Wyn's mouth dropped open. Automatically his eyes flew to the closed door, as though he wanted to confirm that nobody was listening. "You're certain about that?"

"Those places are pretty discreet, but I used the phone number you gave me, indicating it was given me by Virginia Redgrave, and I needed to speak to Charlie concerning a family matter. He's not there, nor has he been there, according to the nurse in charge."

Wyn leaned back in his chair, staring into space, absently steepling his hands before him. "Why would she lie to me?"

"Don't you think that might be obvious?" Michael asked, sipping his coffee.

Suddenly, Wyn bolted out of the chair and started for the door.

"Wait! What are you going to do?" Michael called after him.

"I'm going to confront Virginia. This company has been good to her for many years. How could she do this to us? Why didn't she just ask for a loan?"

Michael watched Wyn pace back and forth before the closed door. His face was turning a dark red, as if he were struggling to hold his temper, although he was not succeeding.

"I don't advise you to say anything to her yet. We have to talk about this some more. The fact that he didn't check into the hospital doesn't guarantee that he grabbed Mary. We're treading on thin ice here, Wyn."

Wyn had been staring dazedly at the floor, but now his head jerked up. "What do you mean?"

"You can't just confront her that way. If she's a link to Mary, we have to be careful with her. Very careful."

Wyn crossed the room and slumped into his chair again. "What do you suggest?"

"If her son is involved in this, she won't voluntarily turn him in, or she would have done that already."

"The other thing that puzzles me is why she wouldn't respond to the reward I've offered." Wyn's eyes searched Michael's face. "If this were just about money, why haven't they just left her someplace and called in for the reward? I mean, I see people do that on television."

For a moment Michael was touched by this businessman, so astute in running his company yet so naive in matters of the heart.

"Because there's a reason for waiting. That alone may back up our theory that someone in her department took her. Either she's been blindfolded the entire time or there's a middleman involved, a person hired to abduct her. That would be my guess."

"And just how long do you guess this abduction will continue?" Wyn pressed.

Michael hesitated. He couldn't tell him what he gravely feared. That Mary was no longer alive to identify the person and that the kidnapper was merely biding his or her time to either demand money or give information for the reward.

Wyn glanced at his watch. "My appointment is due here any minute. What do you plan to do next?"

"I'm going to follow through on the Redgrave boy. Also, I meant to ask you. What is Mary's blood type? Do you happen to know?"

Wyn's brow arched. "It's easy to remember because it's rare. B negative. What does that have to do with anything?"

"Just something I wanted to know," Michael said, although he knew the answer didn't satisfy Wyn, whose secretary was already knocking on the door.

"Are you staying in town another night?" he asked.

"Yes, we'll be at the hotel," Michael confirmed. "Try not to worry too much. I'll do the best I can to find Mary for you."

Something flickered in Wyn's eyes for a moment, then passed on. His shoulders slumped as he heaved a deep sigh. "Thanks."

After leaving Wyn's office, they went to the accounting department. As usual, everyone looked busy. When they entered, Virginia Redgrave gave Michael another questioning stare, and he was tempted to stop and ask her the question uppermost in his mind. He resisted the impulse and moved on back to Mary's desk. Elizabeth followed, speaking to Claire.

"Hi," Claire said, and smiled at both of them. "How's it going?"

"Better," Michael said, glancing toward Sue Wilkens's empty chair.

Claire followed his eyes and leaned forward. "She's sick today."

"Oh. Think we could talk to Mrs. McCreary?"

"I'll see." Claire got up and went to the back office, stuck her head in the door, then motioned Michael and Elizabeth back.

"Good morning," Mrs. McCreary said with a smile, coming to her feet as they entered. It looked as though another five pounds of paperwork had been added to her desktop.

"I know you're busy," Michael said, "but this will only take a minute."

"All right." She walked past them to close the door. Then she returned to her desk as they took seats opposite her. "Have you learned anything?" she asked, her eyes as haggard as they were yesterday.

Michael hesitated. "It depends. What do you know about Virginia Redgrave and her son?"

She sighed. "Virginia has had all sorts of problems with him. I gave a great deal of thought to that last night," she said staring at her desk, "but I honestly don't believe Virginia would be involved in Mary's disappearance in any way."

"I'm more suspicious of the son. How old is he?"

"Charlie?" She sighed. "He's around twenty, I think. Barely made it through high school, flunked out of college, then quit trade school. Ran in the wrong crowd."

"You see, those are important words. The wrong crowd could influence him to do something he wouldn't do on his own, if he's addicted to drugs."

"Yes, I know." Mrs. McCreary was looking through the glass window to Virginia. "Would you like me to call Virginia in here?"

Michael hesitated. "Wyn wanted to confront her just now,

158

but he was angry. I thought it was best to wait. And I don't think it's a good idea to call her in here when it's obvious we're investigating."

"Of course. That's very thoughtful of you, because it would be embarrassing to Virginia to be singled out in the presence of her coworkers. Why don't you go down to the cafeteria; then after you leave, I'll quietly ask Virginia to meet you there."

"That's a good idea," Elizabeth said, looking at Michael.

Michael nodded, coming to his feet. "In the meantime, I'd like you to check on one more thing for me."

"All right. What's that?"

"I need to know the blood type on Sue Wilkens's daughter who needs the kidney transplant."

Mrs. McCreary hiked an eyebrow and ran a hand over her short red hair. "She called in sick today, but I could telephone her at home and say that we're updating medical records in the fund we're building for her daughter."

"Good. I would appreciate that. We'll go on to the cafeteria."

They walked casually back through the accounting department, waving to Claire and deliberately ignoring Virginia Redgrave.

Five minutes later, as they faced Virginia across the table in the cafeteria, she folded her hands and looked them squarely in the eye. At close range, she was older than Michael had assumed, late forties, with bitter gray eyes and a lived-in face.

"What's this about?" she asked bluntly.

Michael was equally direct. "In trying to locate Mary Chamblis I'm having to explore every possible motive for her disappearance."

"And since my son Charlie's reputation is in question, you

think he might have kidnapped her?" she asked, ner gray eyes narrowing. "I assume that was why Mr. Dalton called and asked me where Charlie was."

"And he's in Nashville in a rehab clinic?" Michael asked carefully.

"You know he's not," she sighed, as she looked down at her long fingers, laced tightly on the table. "I called right after you did—I assume it was you—and learned that he never checked in. I called his best friend, who had sworn to me that he would drive him there and take care of the details. Well, they never made it," she sighed. "Charlie is in Sevierville with his girlfriend."

"Sevierville?" Elizabeth repeated, glancing at Michael. They both were thinking that Sevierville was not far from Angel Valley...or Painted Rock.

"Before you draw any conclusions, he and his girlfriend were in Knoxville the day Mary disappeared." She gave Michael a sharp glance. "If you had just come to me and asked, I would have told you." She spoke in a flat, bitter tone, with a weariness that indicated she had been questioned often about her son.

"Want to give me the name of his girlfriend?"

She sighed. "Betsy Wilmore. She's in the phone directory under B. J. Wilmore. She works at one of the outlet shops, so I don't know if she's home. I think the name of the apartment building where she lived is Landfield, no, Landmark."

While Michael was making notes, Elizabeth reached forward and touched her hand. "You've done everything you can to help us, Mrs. Redgrave. We'll relay that to Mr. Dalton."

The hazel eyes softened, and for a moment, there was the hint of tears forming. "Charlie didn't do this," she said in a hoarse voice.

"Since we're speaking frankly—" Michael looked up from his notebook—"would you care to speculate on who might have done it? Mary's been missing long enough now to suggest that someone may have taken her life."

Virginia nodded. "Since we're speaking so frankly, I'll say what nobody else has had the guts to say. Wyn Dalton has a nasty temper. Once I passed him and Mary at the end of the hall. He was furious with her about something. When she came in, she was as pale as a ghost. I went back to her desk to see if she was all right, and she pretended that she was. But her hands were shaking."

Michael and Elizabeth exchanged startled glances.

"Naturally I'd like what I've said to be kept confidential. Particularly since he's the man who hired you. I've just always found it a bit strange that they went off together that day and she supposedly fell off Painted Rock."

Michael stared at her. "*Supposedly?*"

"Supposedly," she repeated, meeting his eyes directly.

"Do you think it's possible Mary may have had a little push to help her over that rock?"

She shrugged. "I don't know that I'd go that far with it. I can only tell you what I know. And I do know he was verbally abusive to her. Maybe that's all he ever was."

"But she loved him?" Elizabeth asked, stunned by this news.

"Yes," she sighed, "she must have. Why else do you stay on in a situation like that? I know." She dropped her eyes. "I've been down that same road, only one day I came to my senses and told Charlie's dad to hit the road. He did. We never saw him again."

The three of them sat silently for a moment, lost in their own thoughts. Elizabeth was the first one to speak. "But you don't honestly think Wyn's capable of…doing anything to harm Mary. After all, he's offering a reward, and he's obviously sick with worry."

She shrugged. "He might be sick with worry that his reputation and that of the Dalton Corporation are in jeopardy."

Michael was tapping his pen against the notebook, looking thoughtfully at Virginia. Was she trying to steer them away from Charlie, or did her words ring true? The theory was certainly worth investigating.

"What you've told us will remain confidential, believe me."

"You know I could lose my job over this?"

"I know. And that's why I'm promising confidentiality. But remember something—those words could help us find Mary Chamblis, and I can see that you care about her."

"I do. Very much. She was such a sweet girl." This time the tears she had held at bay filled her eyes, but she turned away, coming to her feet. She was obviously a woman who had known great pain and was accustomed to dealing with it.

"Thanks again," Elizabeth said. "I know this was difficult for you."

She merely nodded, then straightened her back and walked out of the cafeteria.

Elizabeth and Michael turned to stare at each another.

"Well." Elizabeth swallowed. "What do you make of that?"

"I'm taking it seriously, of course. But I'm not getting sidetracked from Charlie, either. I think it's time we checked out of the hotel and headed back to the mountains. Our first stop will be Sevierville. I'll leave word with Wyn's secretary that we'll call him tonight."

Elizabeth nodded, coming to her feet. "Michael, this is a crazy business." Her brown eyes were filled with dismay. "I don't see how you handle it so well."

"I haven't always. What do you think our separation was all about?"

She tiptoed up and kissed him. "I love you," she said tenderly.

"And I love you. Now, let's get back up to the mountains."

As they drove, Michael recalled what Ben had told him about the area. "I understand that Sevierville was once just a friendly little east-Tennessee town, but now it's one of the fastest-growing resort communities in Tennessee."

Elizabeth studied the Dollywood theme park they were passing. "This is one of those times I'd like to forget work and just have fun." She sighed, staring at Dolly Parton's statue on the courthouse square.

"And we will have fun. We're doing too much work, and I'm sorry about that."

"Oh, I'm not," she turned to him, wide-eyed. "We have to find Mary." She smiled. "Then we'll have fun. So where is the Landmark?"

"The guy at the service station said it's just around the next block—2110. A tan frame building, so be on the lookout."

The building came into view as soon as they turned the corner. Elizabeth nodded and pointed. "That's it." Michael slowed the Blazer, pulling in at the curb.

It was a small apartment building in a low-income area. He cut the engine and looked across at Elizabeth. "Coming?"

"What do you think?"

He merely chuckled as they got out and walked up to the building. The mailboxes indicated that B. J. Wilmore and S. T. Thompson were in 214. They climbed the stairs to the upper landing and located the numbers 214 on the first door to the left.

The sound of rock music drifted from inside as Michael knocked on the door. There was no answer. He knocked again, and the music was turned down. Slowly the door opened. A young woman in a short, disheveled T-shirt and cut-off jeans came to the door. Her dark hair was slightly mussed, and the pupils of her blue eyes were dilated.

"Hi. Are you Betsy?" Michael asked.

She looked from Michael to Elizabeth. "No, I'm Sandy. Betsy is my roommate."

"Is she here?"

"She's at work."

Michael tried to see over her head into the apartment, but she managed to block the door.

"Sandy, we're looking for Charlie. His mother gave us this address. We need to talk with him."

The blue eyes grew wider as she looked from Elizabeth to Michael. She opened the door and glanced over her shoulder. "Come in."

The tiny apartment was a mess, but what was even more disappointing to Michael was the sight of Charlie half-asleep on the sofa. From the indented area, Michael guessed that Sandy had occupied the small empty space beside him.

"Charlie." Sandy went over to shake him. "Charlie, wake up."

He rolled over and sat up, blinking sleepily. His hair was the same auburn color as his mother's, and the features of his whiskered face were good. He was, in fact, handsome. He was bare chested and barefooted, wearing only a pair of light gray sweat pants. He blinked and looked at Elizabeth and Michael, then struggled to his feet. His eyes looked even worse than Sandy's, and there was no doubt that he had something other than weariness in his eyes. He had the look of one who uses drugs, Michael concluded.

"Charlie, I'm Michael Calloway, and this is my wife, Elizabeth. I'm a private detective, and I'm working on a case for Wyn Dalton."

This news brought Charlie fully awake. Clearly puzzled, he merely nodded and extended a hand. "Nice to meet you."

At least his mother had taught him to be polite, Michael thought, briefly shaking his hand.

"We need to talk with you about a very serious matter."

He mumbled a curse and sank to the sofa. "I'm gonna check in next week," he said, dropping his face to his hands. "Tell Mom I'm sorry. I just hated the thought of being locked up again. And she shouldn't blame Todd. We started for Nashville bu..." He removed his hands and forced his eyes up to Michael. "I told him to turn around. I wasn't going."

Michael felt an odd mixture of anger and compassion. "I don't have a son," he said, taking a chair opposite the sofa, "but if I did, it would break my heart to see him in the condition you're in. In addition to the drugs, you've got another problem."

Sandy was backing into the kitchen, trying to quietly disappear.

"I'd say you have more than one," Elizabeth blurted before she could stop herself. She was staring with disgust at Sandy's rumpled clothing, and the girl blushed beneath her stare and fled to the next room.

Charlie was sober enough to follow her eyes, glance over his shoulder at Sandy, and get the message. "Yeah, I know. I'm one disgusting mess. It's like I'm on a roller coaster and can't get off. And Betsy really cares about me. I don't know why."

"What about you? Don't you care what you're doing to yourself and to your mother?"

Tears filled his blue eyes now and spilled down his cheeks. "I know. I hate myself." He brushed impatiently at his eyes, then tilted his head and looked curiously at Michael. "What did you mean about *another* problem?"

"Mary Chamblis," Michael said, watching him carefully.

Charlie's back straightened, and he stared at Michael as though he had reached across and slapped him. "Mary Chamblis?" he croaked. "Why would she be a problem for me?"

"Maybe you can explain that to us. Your mother didn't send us here to check on you for skipping out. We came on a lead that you might know something about Mary's disappearance."

He bolted to his feet, nearly stumbling over the coffee table, and muttering another curse.

"Watch your mouth," Michael snapped.

Charlie looked at Elizabeth. "I'm sorry." He took a deep breath that seemed to shake his entire body. He was thin, almost gaunt, and Michael knew the drugs would kill him if he didn't get help soon.

"Why in the—" He glanced at Elizabeth and shut his mouth. He raked through his tousled hair. "Why would you ask me about Mary Chamblis? Man, I wouldn't mess with her. She's Dalton's woman."

"And she's been missing for over four weeks."

Charlie listened, staring intently at Michael. He had been bolted out of his drug-induced stupor by Michael's words. A mixture of comprehension, confusion, then dismay crossed his face as the impact of Michael's statement began to penetrate his senses. He sank onto the sofa, as though his legs could no longer hold him up. "Wait a minute. You don't think…I mean, does Mr. Dalton think…?"

"He isn't sure what to think. I'd suggest you get yourself into a clinic as soon as possible and get your head straight. You're going to have some questions to answer."

"Man, are you serious? What questions? I don't know anything about Mary's disappearance. Who said I did?"

"You could use some money, right? And you know who has money. You also know he'd pay a lot to get her back."

For a moment Charlie looked too stunned to respond, or else he was a good actor. Something broke in the back room.

"Can we look around?" Michael asked, glancing toward a closed door.

"Don't you have to have a search warrant for that?" he asked, an edge to his tone.

"I can get one."

He waved aside the threat. "Go ahead. All you'll find is a mess."

Charlie was telling the truth about the state of their living conditions, Michael quickly discovered, as he checked out the tiny one-bedroom apartment. Sandy was sprawled on one of the twin beds, staring at the ceiling. She looked horrified when he entered.

"Listen, mister, we don't know anything about Mary Chamblis."

"You don't?" Michael asked coolly, opening the closet door and dodging as a shoe box tumbled out. There was scarcely enough room in the closet for clothes, let alone Mary. He closed the door. "Then your only worry is getting your friend into a clinic. And you might want to join him," Michael added, taking another look at her.

Elizabeth and Michael were both opening doors, looking around. It was obvious that Mary was not here.

Charlie had come fully to his senses and was now trailing around after them. His eyes bulged as he, too, peered into possible hiding places as though making sure he had not actually kidnapped Mary and forgotten. "Man, I just can't believe that anyone would think that I—" Charlie broke off, staring wildly into space.

"Get checked into that clinic, Charlie. And stop throwing away your life."

He looked at Michael. "Yes sir. This time I will. Tell Mom I'll ask Betsy to drive me to Nashville tonight—"

"No, you tell her. And this time try to keep your word."

"I will." He nodded solemnly, dropping his head as tears threatened..

"We'll be calling to see that you do," Michael warned. "And, Charlie," Michael added softly, "you aren't going to find happiness in a handful of pills or at the bottom of a bottle. The kind of inner peace you search for can only be found with God."

Charlie merely nodded, never lifting his eyes from the floor.

Elizabeth had said nothing. She merely opened her purse, removed a small pink book of the Psalms and left it on the coffee table. With his head still lowered, Charlie's eyes inched toward the book in silence as they left the apartment.

Neither Michael nor Elizabeth spoke until they were back in the car. Then Michael looked at her as he turned the key in the ignition. "Pretty pathetic, huh?"

She nodded. "Are you going to talk to Betsy?"

He shook his head. "There's no need. He didn't do it."

Elizabeth's mouth fell open. "How do you know?"

"He's in no shape to pull it off."

"What about that 'bad crowd' his mother mentioned?"

"That's a long shot. For now, I want to get back to the chalet and make some phone calls. I've got a couple of ideas."

"Care to share those ideas?" she asked, jabbing him in the ribs.

He flinched from her gesture, turned to give her a grin, then glanced at the approaching red light. "My first and best idea is a candlelight dinner with the most beautiful woman in the world."

Elizabeth laughed. "That's not really what you were thinking."

"No, but it's what we're going to do."

When they returned to the chalet, there were two telephone messages from Ben. He had called yesterday afternoon and again last night. Michael picked up the phone and dialed his number. There was no answer.

Elizabeth peered over his shoulder. "Wonder what Ben wants?"

"Maybe he has some news. Want to rest awhile then have that nice dinner I mentioned earlier? We haven't eaten all day."

"A good plan," she agreed.

He laughed and reached for her. "On the way to dinner we'll stop by the boardinghouse where Ben lives. Maybe on one of his mountain treks, he's stumbled onto something," he said, then winced. "Bad choice of words."

Elizabeth nodded, rolling her eyes.

TEN

On their way to dinner, Michael spotted Ben's truck parked in front of a shop in Angel Valley. He wheeled to the curb. Ben was just coming out with a package. He waved and hurried to Michael's side of the Blazer.

"Hey, you two. Where've you been?" Ben grinned at them. His blond hair was slightly tumbled, as usual, and he was sporting at least three days of whiskers, but he was as affable as always.

"In Knoxville. We're still chasing down leads on Mary Chamblis. Heard anything?"

"No, I haven't. And I did ask around. In fact, I went into Raven's shop to see if she had heard anything."

"Oh?" Elizabeth glanced at Michael. "And had she?"

He shook his head. "No, she hadn't. But she will let us know if she hears anything at all that might be helpful. She's really nice," he added. Then his eyes drifted somewhere over their heads, and he stared into space for a moment.

Michael glanced at Elizabeth and winked. Elizabeth looked back at Ben and smiled. It was obvious to both of them that Ben was infatuated with Raven.

Michael cleared his throat. "Well, I guess—"

"Wait." Ben came back to the moment. "There might be something to check out, although we need to consider the source."

"What is it?" Michael was instantly on the alert.

Ben glanced around, then leaned closer to Michael. "Millie said somebody thought they saw a blond woman with Buster Stringfellow."

Elizabeth's mouth fell open, and yet she was the first to respond. "Where? When?"

"Just this week. It's the local buzz that Buster's got himself a girlfriend. I hear Jasper and the sheriff are having a good laugh over that."

"It may not be a laughing matter," Michael said, staring at Ben. "Why didn't we see some sign of her when we watched that house for hours through the binoculars? And when we got within yelling distance of the cabin, why didn't she come out?"

Ben shrugged. "Good question. Maybe she couldn't come out. But you know we ordered all that honey. Wanna go pick it up in the morning?"

"I certainly do," Michael said, automatically turning to glance down the street toward the post office. Had Millie struck gold for them? He glanced back at Ben. "Why don't you come on over to my place when you're ready."

"Seven too early?" Ben asked. "I'm going on to Cherokee afterwards."

"To see Raven?" Elizabeth teased.

"Yeah, she's a terrific lady."

Elizabeth arched an eyebrow. Ben was bringing his feelings out into the open now. She smiled at him, comprehending. "I want to meet her," she said, noting the gleam in Ben's eye.

"Okay. I'll try to arrange a dinner date for the four of us. She's pretty busy, though. She's really into her work."

"She does stop to eat, doesn't she?" Michael teased.

"Yeah, in fact she nibbles all the time."

Michael started the engine. "You just reminded us that we're starved. See you in the morning at seven."

Ben hesitated. "Do you think this is dangerous? Should we get the sheriff to go with us?"

Michael thought about it. "Not if he and Jasper are laughing about it. Let's check it out one more time. See if we can get inside the house, or at least get close enough for a peep. If anything looks suspicious, then we'll go to Sheriff Grayson."

"You don't think the fact that Buster Stringfellow was seen with a blond warrants enough suspicion to bring in the sheriff?" Elizabeth looked horrified.

"No crime in that," Ben chuckled, oddly at ease with the matter.

"Depends on who the blond was," Michael said, hating the thought of Mary trapped with the Stringfellows. Still, there was hope now that she might still be alive.

"See you at seven, then." Ben stepped back from the Blazer and waved them on.

Michael glanced at Elizabeth. "When I check in with Wyn tonight, maybe I can give him a little bit of hope."

True to his word, Ben was at Michael's door at five minutes till seven. He was freshly shaven and wore a thick sweater and jeans and his standard hiking boots. "Sorry, no biscuit this time," he whispered, peering into the darkness behind Michael.

"That's fine. I ate too much last night anyway. I do have a thermos of coffee to take along with us."

"So do I. We should be pretty wired by the time we get to the Stringfellow cabin."

Michael grabbed his jacket and the thermos and closed the sliding glass door. Again, daylight was just beginning to break, and the crisp mountain air was like a tonic to his senses. After a great dinner and a good night's rest, he was ready to tackle the case with new enthusiasm.

"I talked with Wyn Dalton last night," he said as they climbed into Ben's truck. "Updated him on what I've learned."

"Which is?"

"I have a couple of leads, but I don't have that gut feeling that usually takes over when I'm onto something."

Ben reached over and started the engine, then glanced back at Michael. "You really get a gut feeling?" he asked. "That's interesting."

"Yep, but I'm not always on target. And yet sometimes instinct is all I have to go on."

Ben backed the truck out and turned toward the main highway. "What's your instinct on the Stringfellows?"

Michael sighed. "I'll tell you for sure later. Right now I'm trying to keep an open mind."

"Do you have any objections to our taking the easy route this time?" Ben asked.

"There's an easy way to get to the Stringfellow place?" Michael hiked an eyebrow at him.

"An old forestry road that—"

"Oh, *that* one." Michael nodded. "We tried it, got halfway down, and gave up."

"Bet you got as far as that wide bend in the road and turned around."

"How'd you guess?"

He chuckled. "That's what most people do. What they don't realize is, the road widens out farther down. Once you get to the valley, it's fairly smooth traveling for a truck. When the Stringfellows come out in their pickup, they cross the valley to the far end. There's a short one-laner that leads up to the main highway. It would really be out of the way for us, but safer. We're not likely to encounter any traffic either. Nobody travels it. Probably too afraid they'll meet Buster and have to back all the way out. Buster doesn't budge."

Michael took a breath. "I hope he'll budge today." He

tapped his billfold. "I've got enough in my hip pocket to at least make him blink." He uncorked the thermos, thinking they'd better start revving up their energy. "'Elizabeth is just craving some sourwood honey. Says she can't wait much longer. Does that sound convincing?"

"You bet. Especially since you bought a case of Betty Sue's sassafras tea." He grinned.

"Betty Sue?"

"She has an herb shop in Angel Valley."

Michael had just taken a sip of coffee when they hit the first pothole in the narrow road and more coffee ended up on his sweater than in his mouth.

"Oops, sorry about that," Ben said. "Better hold tight."

"Yeah, I better." He tightly corked the thermos and peered over the dashboard. The narrow road was canopied with tree cover, absorbing the lingering darkness. Ben's headlights were like twin spotlights bobbing up and down over deep potholes. Even peering over the dash, Michael could only guess at the graveled, snake-like road. "I'm glad you're familiar with this particular road," Michael said, hoping he sounded more confident that he felt.

"I'm very familiar with it. So don't worry."

"Sure." Michael gave him a wry grin. He placed his right hand on the door handle and braced himself against the dashboard with his left hand. The truck jumped and bounced and swerved until finally the road smoothed out and eventually widened, as Ben had predicted.

Michael heaved a sigh of relief that sent muscles relaxing all the way to his toes. "For the first time in my life I have a new appreciation for the tangle of interstates curving around Atlanta."

Ben laughed. "Not me. I love this country. Could stay here forever."

Michael looked across at him, searching his happy face. He could see that Ben really meant what he said. "Well, I guess it could be a pretty good life. You can write about these people, and, of course, you can court Raven. What's she really like?" he asked curiously.

The gleam in Ben's eyes brightened as the early morning light spreading over the valley filtered into the truck. "Raven is…," he paused, as though wanting to get every word right. "She's intelligent, interesting, and really into the history of her people. I could talk to her forever."

"Maybe you will," Michael said, looking over the features of Ben's face and wondering if the guy had any idea how he lit up like neon when Raven's name was mentioned.

Ben glanced quickly at Michael and shook his head. "Oh, I'm not that far along with things. I just like her a lot, but I still don't know her very well."

"Mmm-hmm," Michael commented, thinking that the fact that Ben didn't know her very well had not altered his attraction to her in the least; if anything, he was more intrigued than ever.

"One thing I appreciate about her is the way she listens, really listens. You know how some women pretend to be interested in what you're saying but then you catch them looking out the window or stifling a sigh. Raven looks at me…differently."

"Maybe she's got it as bad as you."

Ben chuckled. "I doubt that. Well, get ready. We're approaching the Stringfellow property." So far no bullets were zipping over the truck, which gave them hope.

Ben began to toot his horn as they approached the cabin, and a flop-eared hound loped around a corner of the house, tossed his head back, and went into a series of ear-splitting howls.

The front door burst open, and one of the younger Stringfellow men hurtled out, shotgun in hand.

"Wave and look friendly," Ben warned through his teeth as his lips stretched back in a huge smile.

Michael waved and smiled as well, as another head came to the door. More backup, Michael assumed.

The younger Stringfellow was less bushy than Buster and appeared less inclined to aim the shotgun.

Ben slowed down until the truck was barely crawling toward the house. He rolled down the window. "Buster told us to come back to pick up some honey."

The frown never disappeared from the face of the man on the porch, but the shotgun lowered a fraction of an inch.

A loud voice erupted in the background, and big Buster bounded onto the porch. Both men wore overalls without shirts, and just the size of their brawny arms was threat enough for Michael. He wondered why they needed a shotgun. He reminded himself to later congratulate Ben on his courage, for Ben rolled the window down even farther when Buster appeared.

"Buster, we've come after the honey."

"Just hold it right there." Buster jabbed a thick finger toward them.

Ben stopped the truck but wisely left the engine running.

Buster turned around and mumbled something to the other brother, who went back inside. Then, to their amazement, a tiny woman in jeans, oversized sweatshirt, and gray hair slicked back in a tight bun stepped onto the porch. She was obviously the brains of the outfit because after she mumbled something to Buster, he lumbered down the steps toward the truck.

"Pull up and back in so we can load the honey," he commanded.

Michael heard Ben's sigh of relief as he nodded and did as he was told, careful not to get too near the house. Michael decided if he was ever going to be bold about this, now was the time to make his move.

Sending up a quick prayer for his safety, he got out of the truck.

"What're you doing?" Buster barked.

"Just thought I'd help load the honey," he said innocently. He gave the old woman his most charming smile. "Ma'am, my wife just loves sourwood honey. We really appreciate your selling us some."

"Hard to get good honey." Her voice was as tweaky as a bird's note, and she glared at him as she spoke.

Buster nodded. "That's right. Ma makes the best. It took us two days to get those hives robbed. Wilbur got stung twice."

Poor bee, thought Michael, but he wagged his head in sympathy. "Don't know how you guys do that."

"It ain't easy," Buster boasted, looking Michael over. "Where you from?"

"Atlanta. You can't get good honey in Atlanta," he said, looking again at the little woman and sensing she would be his best ally. "Ma'am, I bet you can make biscuits better than any woman in these parts. In fact, if you feed these guys some biscuits with a mouthful of your honey—" he shook his head— "well, they just don't know how lucky they are."

Buster's eyes on him widened as the birdlike woman inched another step forward.

"Yore woman don't make biscuits," Birdie accused.

"I haven't had a decent biscuit since my grandmother died."

"Then you stay right there," she twirped at him.

Michael froze in his tracks, not daring to disobey. If there was one thing that was apparent to him, it was that the "boys" here appreciated good cooking. No doubt the reason the little woman was so thin was because she slaved in the kitchen twenty hours a day.

"You gonna help me, Buster?" the other brother growled as he lugged out a huge cardboard box. "Don't want the bottom to fall out of the box while I'm toting these jars of honey."

"Here, I'll help you," Michael offered, bounding onto the front porch and praying the shotgun wouldn't go off in his face.

He was close enough to smell them, and it was not a pleasant odor, but in the process his eyes darted through the open door. He had a clear view of scuffed wooden floors, wooden furniture that looked handmade…and the tips of a woman's shoes. She was sitting in a chair near the door.

"We don't need you to help," Buster said, taking offense.

Michael was backing away when the little woman came out with a fluffy biscuit. "You kin try it," she said, shoving it in his face.

Michael looked at the huge brown biscuit, wondering about the cleanliness of the kitchen and exactly what ingredients went into the object in his hand. Still, he couldn't back down now. He took a big bite and rolled his eyes heavenward. He chewed slowly, closing his eyes. When he opened them, Buster was peering down into his face as though Michael had lost his mind.

"These are even better than my grandmother's biscuits, God rest her soul," Michael said. *Only better because Granny's home-made jam wasn't inside the biscuit,* he silently amended.

"Shame when a fellow can't even get a good biscuit nowadays," Birdie replied, obviously distressed.

The honey had been loaded into the truck, and Michael knew time was running out. He darted a desperate glance toward the tips of those shoes, still visible at the edge of the door. They were black and soft, like house shoes.

"Oh, I almost forgot. Let me pay you," he said, reaching for his back pocket.

The shotgun came up, centered on his forehead.

"I have to get my wallet," he said with a smile, trying not to notice how unfriendly these people tended to be.

"Wilbur, get that gun outa the man's face!" the little woman screeched.

At that the shoes moved, and Michael took his time reaching into his wallet. He had been careful not to bring more than he could afford parting with, so in one grand gesture, he handed Buster four twenties. He figured one biscuit had cost him at least one of those twenties.

Both brothers and Birdie stared at the money. The little woman's mouth curled in what Michael assumed was a grin of satisfaction.

"Do you think I could have just one more biscuit before we go?" he asked, giving the woman his most pleading look.

"Reckon so."

"Caroline," Buster yelled, "bring this man a biscuit. Ma, you be sure you've counted out those jars of honey right."

Michael's eyes lingered on the woman's shoes, wondering what he could do to get inside the house. Ben had found his voice and was responding. "Oh, don't bother. I'm sure it's right. We'll just be on our way now."

"Not yet," the little woman screeched, glancing over her shoulder.

The front door opened wider and a blond woman stepped out holding a biscuit. She was a sturdy woman in her thirties with short bleached-blond hair and a face pockmarked from acne. She handed him a biscuit and gave Michael a wide grin. At least half of her teeth were missing.

ELEVEN

So now we've met Buster's girlfriend," Ben said on a sigh as he drove slowly away from the cabin, with half a dozen eyes watching their bouncing departure. "It's great how you're making friends with them."

"Yeah," Michael said, staring glumly at the road. The biscuit was curled in the palm of his hand, all but forgotten. *"You're* making friends with them. I don't think I care to go back."

"But just think of the mountain stories they can tell."

He nodded. "And you can put them all in your book. That way it won't be a complete waste of your time."

"Or your money! Michael, you're not paying me for this trip; I should be paying you. I've been wanting a chance to talk with the Stringfellows."

"Well, good luck with them," Michael said, shaking his head. When they were a safe distance from the Stringfellow house, he rolled the window down and tossed the biscuit out.

"Really, Michael, you don't realize it, but they were actually friendly compared to the way they treat other people."

Michael snorted. "Maybe it's because we didn't ask to see their special little garden out back."

"Yeah, I forgot about that," Ben sighed. "But you didn't hear it from me."

The day that had dawned so bright and full of promise was slowly turning cloudy. The sun had disappeared behind a large gray cloud, matching the gloom that threatened Michael. He hadn't realized how much hope he had placed in the rumor of a blond at the Stringfellow cabin until now. All roads to Mary seemed to be coming to a dead end.

Ben drove slowly, taking care not to jostle all the honey jars out of the back of the truck. It seemed to take forever to get back to the chalet. When at last they pulled into the driveway, Michael saw he wasn't the only one whose hopes were riding on the rumor of a blond.

Wyn Dalton's sleek Mercedes sports vehicle was parked out front. He and Elizabeth were seated on the porch, but at the sight of Michael and Ben, Wyn jumped to his feet. His eyes narrowed, searching the front seat. Then his shoulders slumped when he realized Mary was not with them.

"Looks like you have company," Ben commented.

"Yeah, I shouldn't have told him about the rumor of a blond at the Stringfellow cabin when we talked last night."

"You were just doing your job," Ben said, pulling to a halt.

Michael hopped out of the truck. "Wyn, you didn't need to make a trip up here; I would have called you."

Wyn nodded. "I just hoped…" His voice trailed off.

"There was a blond woman at the Stringfellow cabin all right," Michael confirmed. "But she's a far cry from your Mary."

Ben slammed his door and approached them, chuckling. "She looks like she fell out of the ugly tree and hit every branch going down."

"Ben," Elizabeth scolded, half smiling, "that was unkind."

Watching Wyn, Michael could see that he was not amused by the remark.

Michael turned and made the introductions, but Wyn was reserved in his greeting.

"I made coffee and tea about twenty minutes ago when Wyn arrived. You guys want something?"

"We have plenty of honey to go into the tea," Ben said,

pointing to the load. "Thanks to Michael, we're the only strangers they've allowed on their front porch."

"Oh good, I can put real honey in my tea."

Wyn placed his hands on his hips and looked from Elizabeth to Michael to Ben. "You people seem to think this incident is funny," he said stiffly.

Michael's eyes swept over him. In spite of the fact that he was dressed in casual slacks and a button-down shirt, open at the collar, he was unable to soften his rather stuffy nature. He always looked as if he should be dressed in a properly tailored suit, with the latest designer tie looped around his neck.

Michael sighed, unable to control his frustration. "Wyn, I'm too tired to be funny, believe me. In the past forty-eight hours I've scoped Mary's condo like a cat burglar, I've identified Erin Oldham's mysterious boyfriend, I've tracked down and grilled Charlie Redgrave, and now Ben and I risked our lives to get a look at the blond in the Stringfellow cabin. But maybe I'm not moving fast enough for you."

From the corner of his eye he saw Elizabeth's eyes widen in shock, and he sensed that Ben took a step backward. He had a silly flashback to the old western movies where everyone parted for the two gunslingers about to draw. He couldn't help himself for getting smart with Wyn. This was the most difficult case he had ever tried to solve.

Wyn's expression changed. He looked down at his polished, all-leather boots and sighed. "I didn't mean to sound unappreciative. I guess I'm just disappointed," he said, heaving a sigh. "No other leads?" He looked drearily at Michael.

"Just possibilities. But I've told you that if your fiancée can be found, I intend to find her. And I will do just that, if possible. But don't expect the impossible. Maybe the sheriff and the search-and-rescue team did a better job than you thought."

"How could she just vanish into thin air?" Wyn asked with an edge that was starting to wear on Michael's nerves.

"People *don't* just vanish into thin air," Michael said, climbing the porch steps. He didn't care if Wyn joined him in a chair or not. Nor did he offer him one. "There is one theory that has been too horrible to envision, but maybe it's time I told you. There's been a suggestion that she fell and a hungry bear with cubs to feed got to her. Sorry, but I'm just giving you one theory."

Wyn stared at Michael for a moment as though he could not believe what he was hearing. Then, almost imperceptibly, he shook his head as though trying to dispel the image that Michael had cast upon his mind. He lifted his wrist and glanced at his Rolex.

"I'd better get back to town." He looked back at Michael. "Give it another couple of days; then if you don't come up with anything, we'll call it quits."

Michael nodded, biting the inside corner of his lip. "All right, I will. Sorry you drove up for nothing."

Wyn merely shrugged and headed for his car. Then, remembering something, he stopped and looked back at Elizabeth. "Thanks for the coffee," he said, with only the semblance of a smile.

"You're welcome, Wyn," she called as he got into his vehicle and drove off.

Michael, Elizabeth, and Ben stared after him.

"It was nice meeting *you,* too," Ben drawled.

Michael glanced at Ben, who was shaking his head. "I don't particularly like that guy," he said. "I hope he's paying you enough to make this search worthwhile."

"He's paying me well, but this may be one request that money can't buy."

"Are you guys hungry?" Elizabeth asked. "I put on some

vegetable soup soon after you left, Michael. It should be ready now."

Michael was slumped into the porch chair, staring thoughtfully at the mountains.

She looked at Ben. "He isn't listening. What about you, Ben?"

"Vegetable soup sounds terrific to me," Ben said, smiling.

"And we can top it off with a bowl of honey," Michael added caustically.

"Cheer up." Elizabeth tapped him on the shoulder. "I woke up with a good feeling today. I've already said my prayers; looks like now *you* could use a few."

Michael tilted his head back and looked up at her, his eyes filling with love. "Ben, when you find a lady like this one, hang on for dear life." He reached for her hand.

Ben cleared his throat. "It's good to know people like you two find each other."

"Speaking of relationships—" Michael looked back at Ben and smiled for the first time in an hour—"what time are you seeing Raven?"

"I'm heading to Cherokee when I leave here. She happens to be working today. Someone in the shop had a family emergency, and she offered to fill in."

"I'd love to see that shop," Elizabeth said. "Not to intrude on your date, but would it be okay for Michael and me to ride over in our Blazer, say hello to her, and then browse around Cherokee? The only time I've been there was to pick up two exhausted mountain climbers."

Ben laughed, and Michael tried to recapture his own sense of humor.

"Then you definitely need to go back and look around, maybe even tour the reservation," Ben said, looking from Elizabeth to Michael. "I'm sure Raven would like to meet you.

185

It isn't really a date, anyway. As a matter of fact, she doesn't even know that I'm coming," he said with a grin. "But she was telling me about an old Cherokee man who does a special kind of carving. I collect that sort of thing. I wanted her to give me directions on how to locate him."

Michael nodded. "Uh-huh. You might need to work on that line a little before you repeat it to her. You're a bit obvious, fella."

Ben ducked his head, and Elizabeth swatted playfully at Michael. "That sounds perfectly reasonable to me, Ben. And don't pay any attention to Michael. He gets pouty when he can't solve a case in twenty-four hours."

"It's been longer than that."

"Yeah, but I loved the way you laid it out to Wyn Dalton," she laughed. "You guys come and eat so we can devise our next strategy."

Michael tilted his head and looked at her. "You're really enjoying this little chase, aren't you, honey?"

"I'm loving it," she replied quickly. "So hurry up."

After a quick and enjoyable lunch, Elizabeth and Michael got into the Blazer and followed Ben in his truck to Cherokee. It was a beautiful drive, with breathtaking views of mountains and valleys and a feeling of freedom unlike any Elizabeth had known in months.

"Oh, Michael, I'm sorry we're having to make this trip because of poor Mary, but I have to tell you that I absolutely adore this country. It just seems to replenish my soul." Her eyes drifted to the crystal river chattering over smooth rocks and paralleling the road. She rolled down the window inhaling deeply of the fresh mountain air and listening to the incessant gurgle of the water.

Michael glanced at Elizabeth. "I agree with you. This country does seem to replenish the soul. I've always felt an attraction to hang around here." His eyes wandered back to the winding road that had led them through Smoky Mountain National Park and now ended up on the Cherokee reservation. "You see that two-lane that veers off this road to the right up there?"

He pointed to a road that led up a hillside.

She looked to the right. "Yeah, what about it?"

"Raven's cabin is up that road. Well, the cabin itself is not on the road. There's a narrow trail that veers off the road past a couple of old frame houses before you get to her cabin."

Elizabeth hiked an eyebrow. "That road itself looks pretty primitive."

"Not nearly as primitive as the trail where Raven lives, but she seems to love it."

Elizabeth had other questions, as usual, but her attention was quickly captivated by the unique blend of native gift shops and a museum offering authentic Cherokee culture.

"I can't wait to look around here," she said, her eyes glowing at the prospect of an afternoon of shopping.

"I'll leave the shopping to you. I'm trying to remain focused on Mary Chamblis. I just saw one of the posters about her in the front window of that crafts store."

Elizabeth glanced over her shoulder. "Oh, I missed it. Look, Michael." Elizabeth tugged his sleeve. "Over there is the mountainside theater where *Unto These Hills* is being performed. I've always wanted to see that drama."

"Me too. I think I'd enjoy it all the more by watching it here, in the very place that gave refuge to those who weren't taken on the Trail of Tears."

Ben's truck was turning in before one of the small shops, and Michael pulled in and parked beside him.

Elizabeth stretched. "Ah, now I get to meet Raven!"

Michael turned off the engine and winked at Elizabeth. "You'll like her."

They followed Ben into a large shop that featured a wide variety of Native American crafts.

Three salesclerks stood behind counters, but Elizabeth immediately recognized Raven. She was a beautiful woman with shiny black hair that hung in a single braid. Dark bangs brushed her forehead, and her eyes were a deep velvet brown. She had small features, round cheeks, and smooth lips. She wore no makeup, and yet she was striking in her natural beauty, accented by a soft tan dress with fringed sleeves and intricate beadwork around the neck.

Ben made a path straight to her counter. Elizabeth and Michael hung back for a moment, giving them privacy as Elizabeth examined a few interesting baskets. The sign above the baskets advertised them as being authentic, from rivercane with bloodroot dye.

"Michael? Elizabeth?" Ben called to them just as a polite salesclerk approached.

Elizabeth smiled at one of the salesclerks. "Be back in a minute." She slipped her hand in Michael's as they casually strolled back to the glass counter where Ben was pointing to necklaces of intricate beadwork. "Aren't these lovely?"

"Yes, they are," Elizabeth agreed, smiling at the woman behind the counter.

"Raven, you remember Michael. I'd like you to meet Elizabeth."

"Hello." Her lips parted in a half smile as her dark eyes flashed over Elizabeth's jeans and sweatshirt.

"How do you do?" Elizabeth smiled warmly. "It's a pleasure to meet you. Is this your beadwork?" She indicated the patterns neatly displayed in the counter below.

"Some of it," Raven acknowledged. "That on the lower shelf."

Elizabeth nodded. It was very intricately done and quite beautiful. "I like it," she said, smiling back at Raven. "Ben told me you also design dresses. Did you design the one you're wearing?"

She nodded shyly. "Yes, I did. Actually, I'm just learning to design dresses. There seems to be a shortage of authentic styles, so Owl Woman, the oldest Cherokee woman in the area, is taking a few students. I love working with her. In the past I've concentrated on beadwork such as this." She indicated the necklaces, headbands, and coin purses.

"You do beautiful work."

"Thank you. Do you have any word on the blond woman?" she asked Michael.

Michael shook his head. "Afraid not. I don't suppose you've heard anything."

"No. I'm sorry." She looked back at Elizabeth, waiting for her to speak.

"Could I see that necklace?" Elizabeth pointed to a delicate white one.

Raven slid open the glass counter and carefully removed the necklace. She straightened and spread the necklace on the counter.

Elizabeth smiled at her. "You do amazing work."

At the compliment, Raven looked pleased. "This is the work my people have always done. Beadwork and baskets and wood carvings," she explained with pride.

"Speaking of carvings," Ben interjected, "I wanted to ask you about the man who does such good work on the little animals you showed me."

She nodded. "Willie Whitehorse. He is very good. In fact, he brought in some little walnut bears over there." She pointed.

"Wonderful," Ben said, never taking his eyes from Raven's face.

"Oh, over *there?*" Michael repeated, hoping to pry Ben's eyes toward the carvings he had inquired about.

Ben turned slowly, looking somewhat dazed. "Yes, we'll see those in a minute. By the way, Michael and Elizabeth and I wondered if you would join us for an early dinner. Elizabeth is intrigued by the legends of your people."

Elizabeth jumped to the cue. "That's right. Once a month I volunteer to do the story at my daughter's school. She's just going into fourth grade. I'd love to be able to tell them something about your people."

"There are many books available in the area. In fact, just down the street—" she lifted her hand, rippling the fringe on her sleeve—"is a good bookstore."

So much for that, thought Elizabeth. "Well, great. I'll pick up some books."

"We'd like to treat you to dinner," Michael offered.

She hesitated, looking from Elizabeth to Michael to Ben. "I'm sorry. I already put something on the stove when I left this morning. Thank you, anyway."

Ben's mouth literally sagged in disappointment, and Elizabeth couldn't help wondering if Raven noticed.

"Well, I'd like the necklace," Elizabeth said, nudging Michael.

He reached for his wallet. "See anything else?"

"Oh, I'm sure I will," she said, watching Raven carefully wrap the necklace in tissue paper. "This is a wonderful shop," she added as Raven handed the package to her.

A reserved smile touched Raven's mouth again as she studied Elizabeth. "I enjoy working here. There is so much talent among our people."

"I can see that," Elizabeth agreed, wishing they could be friends, but as Ben had predicted, this woman, like many of the others, was more reserved than the slap-them-on-the-back Southerners she and Michael knew back in Atlanta.

Michael paid for the necklace while Ben fidgeted. "Guess I'll go over and take a look at the carvings."

Raven shyly thanked Michael for the purchase; then Elizabeth and Michael wandered with Ben toward the carvings. "Look at this one." Ben indicated a small walnut bear, perfectly carved.

"It's a handsome carving," Michael agreed, glancing toward the window.

There was no poster of Mary Chamblis here, but it didn't seem to matter. He had already spotted one as they entered Cherokee, and he felt certain there would be others. Somehow he didn't think a missing woman from Knoxville really mattered to these people, even though they were polite and caring. Cherokee just seemed to be a world unto itself, needing nothing from the outside world except the money the people earned through their labor.

Ben chose a bear small enough to fit into the palm of his hand. "Perfect," he said, paying for the skillfully carved animal.

"Do you see anything else you want?" Michael looked at Elizabeth.

She shook her head. "I guess not."

Her eyes were drawn back to Raven, who was watching Ben. Elizabeth wandered back toward her counter. "Sure you won't join us?" she asked casually, hoping she wasn't overdoing the invitation.

Raven hesitated, dragging her eyes from Ben. Elizabeth

smiled at her. "My husband is here on a job, but I'm just tagging along having fun. We've just recently met Ben, and he's fallen completely in love with this area." *And you,* she wanted to add.

Slowly Raven's expression changed, became less guarded. "Would you like to share supper with me?" she asked.

"Oh—" Elizabeth glanced toward the men, then back at Raven—"that's very generous of you, but you needn't feel compelled to invite us."

She shrugged. "I'm not. But I do have some handmade items at my cabin that Ben wants to know more about." She was looking at Ben again. "I think it's nice that he wants to write about my people."

"Yes, he's absolutely fascinated," Elizabeth quickly answered, then hoped she wasn't speaking too hastily. She sensed one had to move slowly with this woman, who seemed to see right through to the soul of a person. "We'd enjoy seeing those handmade items too, but we don't want to inconvenience you."

Raven was thoughtful for a moment, then she shook her head. "It won't be an inconvenience. I made a large pot of corn chowder I'd be happy to share."

"Then I'll check with the guys."

Ben, of course, was delighted with the invitation while Michael was somewhat indifferent.

"I really need to snoop around a little," he said under his breath to Elizabeth.

"We can do that later," she mumbled back. "For now, the least we can do is help Ben out. I think he's going to need a little push anyway."

"Sounds good to me." Michael spoke in a clear, distinct voice.

TWELVE

Raven's log cabin was exactly as Michael had described it, Elizabeth thought, studying the house that was centered on the edge of the woods.

Elizabeth and Michael had followed behind Ben's truck, observing the couple through the truck's rear window. Raven was seated on the passenger's side, her dark head turned toward Ben. Ben had obviously dominated the conversation during the three-mile trip, for his right hand kept sweeping the air as though to punctuate his sentences.

"You know," Elizabeth speculated, "I believe she's interested in Ben. I saw the way she looked at him."

"Oh? And just how was that?" Michael teased, parking beneath a pine tree.

"You know the look." Elizabeth smiled at him. "Remember the way I first looked at you? That I'm-interested-tell-me-more kind of look."

"Is that what it's called?"

"That's what I called it."

He chuckled and cut the engine. Ben and Raven were already out of the truck, and Raven was reaching into a black woven bag for her house key. She looked back at them, giving them that shy smile but saying nothing.

"I've noticed she doesn't waste words," Michael said as he reached for the door handle.

"That must be a refreshing treat for you," Elizabeth said under her breath, opening her door.

Once outside, Michael placed his hands on his hips and thoughtfully surveyed the landscape. If someone had passed this trail with a woman in tow, surely Raven would have noticed. He shook his head, coming back to the hungry-bear theory. That seemed like an easy way out of a puzzling situation, but what was left?

"Well, you guys, come on in," Ben called from the open door on the front porch.

Elizabeth tugged at Michael's sleeve. "Give it a rest, Michael. Mary just isn't going to emerge from these woods and solve all your problems."

He nodded. "I know. I think I'll be relieved to give up on this case."

"You won't give up," she replied absently. "I know you too well."

He shrugged and grinned as they climbed the porch steps and entered the cabin.

Elizabeth paused in the doorway, looking around. This was not at all what she had expected, although she wasn't sure exactly what her expectations were. True, it was a log cabin, and it had been here for a very long time. Still, it was warm and inviting. It smelled pleasantly of scented candles and some other aroma that floated to her from the kitchen. Her mouth watered.

The front room was filled with polished wood furniture: a square sofa with thick cushions and a colorful woven blanket tossed over the back, a perfectly round coffee table that had once been a tree trunk, a massive armoire with detailed carvings, a coat tree, a small desk and chair, and a modern sewing machine. A hand-loomed rug overlaid plain wooden floors that looked as though they were waxed daily. Elizabeth almost winced when she thought of her own floors in comparison.

"Make yourselves at home," Raven called to them, indicating the sofa. "I'll slip out of this dress and put on some jeans."

She headed into an adjoining room, leaving Ben standing before the fireplace, admiring the room, and Michael and Elizabeth seated on the sofa.

When Ben turned back to them, Elizabeth gave him a thumbs-up, and he grinned and glanced quickly toward the closed door of the bedroom.

"So, Ben, you're interested in carvings?" Michael asked conversationally.

"Yes, I am. Actually, I'm interested in anything made by the Native Americans or the mountain people. Mom says we're Irish, but I suspect there must be Cherokee blood mixed in with ours somewhere along the line." He looked toward the window. "I feel as if I've come home here in these mountains."

"That's the way I've always felt," Raven spoke up, as she entered the room.

She looked small and slim in the straight jeans and blue sweatshirt. Elizabeth tilted her head and looked at her. Out of her buckskin, she was just another woman, except for the rich darkness of her hair and eyes.

"Tell us about yourself," Elizabeth said, feeling as though she were almost as intrigued as Ben.

Raven turned her dark eyes toward Elizabeth. "What would you like to know?" she asked, in her direct manner.

Elizabeth shrugged. "Well—" she looked around the room—"how long have you lived here? And what's it like being a part of this area that enchants everyone so much?"

"This cabin has been in my family for a hundred years. It offers a kind of peace that I didn't find away at school. It's wonderful," Raven said, following Elizabeth's gaze to the window. "And I know how fortunate I am."

"Tell us about your ancestors."

Raven looked from Michael and Elizabeth to Ben and took a deep breath. "That's a long story. My grandmother married a wild young Scotsman, and together they built this house. Her mother lived here with them until she died. Then my father came to Cherokee and met my mother, and they lived here. It's funny." She looked from Michael to Ben, then back to Elizabeth. "The women have been the ones to continue the family line here in this place. My mother was born in this cabin, grew up here, then married my father, who was Irish."

Elizabeth stared at her thoughtfully. "So you are one-half Irish?"

"In my heart, I am entirely Cherokee. And you will see this is true when we eat the corn chowder."

Ben's smile widened. "Is that what smells so wonderful?"

She nodded and invited them into the kitchen. It was a small room, yet neat and cozy, with a variety of small baskets as wall decorations. The refrigerator and electric stove seemed out of place in this setting.

Raven lifted the lid of a large iron pot and the wonderful aroma that had greeted them at the front door now filled the room. Simple woven place mats adorned the round table, framed by four ladder-back chairs.

"What can I do to help?" Elizabeth offered.

"You can get down the glasses from there." Raven indicated a small cabinet. "I'm afraid all that I can offer for drinks is water or herbal tea."

"Water is fine with me," Ben quickly offered. Michael agreed.

"And I'll take water," Elizabeth joined in, although she would have loved to sample some of Raven's herbal tea. She had noticed several small clay pots on the windowsill above the sink. Sprigs of mint and parsley and other mysterious herbs peeked from the pots.

"There's a pitcher of water in the refrigerator," Raven directed.

Elizabeth opened the refrigerator, which held very little food, so the pitcher containing water was easy to locate. Elizabeth could see that Raven lived quite frugally, and yet she seemed perfectly content, unlike so many other young women her age in the cities, who were always shopping, always restless.

Raven was dipping a wooden spoon into the pot, ladling the steaming chowder into small bowls. Elizabeth peered into the pot and saw, to her relief, that there was plenty of chowder for everyone. "That looks divine."

"Thank you," Raven said, handing her a bowl. She removed a tin of corn muffins from the bread box and passed those around, along with a dish of real butter.

Once they were seated at the table, Michael and Elizabeth glanced at one another, waiting to say grace, but Raven and Ben seemed unaware of their pause. Elizabeth smiled at Michael, closed her eyes momentarily, offering a quick silent prayer, then lifted her spoon.

The chowder was made from a rich cream base with corn, celery, carrots, and onions cooked to just the right tenderness while retaining their crispness. The muffins were thick and chewy, and when Raven suggested they add thick pats of butter, Elizabeth glanced at Raven in fascination.

"How do you stay trim eating such wonderful rich food? I'd be fat!"

Ben chuckled and answered for Raven. "When I was here day before yesterday, she was just taking an apple pie from the oven. In fact, we ate half of it, didn't we?"

Raven nodded, smiling at Ben across the table. Watching

her, Elizabeth recognized the same look of infatuation that seemed to overtake Ben.

"And I finished the other half yesterday," Raven said and looked at Elizabeth. "For once, I don't have a dessert to offer. I'm sorry."

"Please don't apologize," Michael spoke up. "This is the best corn chowder I've ever tasted. No offense, Elizabeth."

"None taken," she laughed. "I've never attempted corn chowder."

"What do you do in Atlanta?" Raven asked her.

"I'm a Christian psychologist," Elizabeth replied.

"A *Christian* psychologist?" Raven looked at her curiously. "I thought all psychologists were the same."

"No," Elizabeth replied, "we're not all the same."

Michael knew she was thinking of Dr. Phillips and that Raven had no way of knowing how painful the subject was for Elizabeth. "Elizabeth is wonderful at her work," he said. "She's very kind and understanding with her clients. A lot of people don't understand what she means when she refers to herself as a Christian counselor, so let me explain. When Elizabeth counsels clients, she does so using Scripture from the Bible as her guide. She's wonderful at her work."

Raven looked puzzled. "I don't understand. How can you counsel clients by using Scripture? I thought you had to apply psychology."

"Well, I do apply the psychology that I learned in college," Elizabeth answered. "But I believe that by adding the spiritual element, people get much better results."

"The spiritual element," Raven repeated, looking at Michael, then Ben. "I'm afraid I don't know much about Christianity. My people had their own spirits, even though we've been exposed to the Christian religion." She shrugged. "Some have chosen it now, and some have not."

There was a moment of awkward silence as Elizabeth's eyes locked with Michael's, and both longed to witness to her. Elizabeth was trying to think of the best way to do that when Ben bridged the gap in conversation.

"Raven, I've told you that I'm describing native beliefs and rituals in my thesis. Sometime I'd like to talk more with you about Cherokee legend and lore."

She nodded. "My people have an interesting legend about how the world was formed that you might include in your thesis," she said to Ben. Then her dark eyes moved to Elizabeth. "I'm sure it differs greatly from your version."

"Maybe not," Elizabeth said around a huge bite of her muffin. "Tell us."

"We'd love to hear it. Really," Ben insisted.

Raven passed the muffins around. "All right. First there were animals and people living in a world above with only water on what we now call earth. When the world above became overcrowded, the water beetle came down here to look around. When he dived deep into the water, he filled his mouth with soft mud; then, returning to the world above, he spit out the mud, and it began to grow so big and so fast that it became an island. The word *earth* was given to the island by the animals.

"The raven was chosen to go down and investigate earth, to see if it was dry enough for the other animals to inhabit. The raven came down and flew around. He became tired, so tired that when he reached the Cherokee lands, his wings started to droop. Wherever his wings struck the ground, a valley was scooped up. When he rose again, a mountain was formed. The mountains and valleys belonging to the Cherokee are credited as coming from the wings of the raven." She hesitated, looking around the table. "The legend goes on, but I can see from your faces that the story sounds quite absurd to you. It's just a legend," she spoke softly.

"Do you believe it?" Elizabeth asked, obviously troubled.

"I believe some of the legends, but no, I'm not sure I believe that particular one."

"Then how do you believe the world was formed?" Elizabeth pressed.

Raven did not answer for a moment, and Michael spoke up.

"Our belief is that God created the world in seven days. There's a very interesting account of it in the Bible. Do you happen to have a Bible?"

Raven shook her head. "No, I don't. Would you like more corn chowder?" she asked smoothly, politely ending the subject.

Elizabeth met Michael's eyes momentarily, then she smiled at Raven. "I'm afraid I can't hold another bite. But thank you so much for inviting us, Raven. This was delicious. May I help you with the dishes now?"

Raven shook her head. "No, I prefer to clean the kitchen later."

"Are you sure we can't help?" Michael asked. "It's impolite to eat and run, but I'm afraid that's what we'll have to do." He lifted his wrist and glanced at his watch. "I'm supposed to be on the job, and I'm afraid I've let myself get sidetracked with my own interests."

"I have enjoyed sharing my meal with you, but I understand if you must leave." Her eyes strayed to Ben, a question in their depths.

"Would you mind if I stayed on a while longer?" Ben asked.

She shook her head, and her single braid swung against her T-shirt. "No, I'd enjoy your company."

"Well in that case—" Michael stood and helped Elizabeth from her chair—"we'll be on our way. We hope to see you again soon, Raven."

Raven made no comment; she merely smiled her reserved smile.

"Thank you so much," Elizabeth said. "And I'll treasure my necklace. As a matter of fact, I wouldn't mind having one of those dresses like you were wearing today. It would be wonderful to wear it when I visit Katie's school and do my program."

Raven looked at her. "I could design one for you, but it will take awhile to complete. When do you plan to return to Atlanta?" Her eyes drifted to Michael.

"Pretty soon," Michael answered. "My employer has only given me two more days to locate Mary Chamblis, and I'm finding it very difficult. Unless I turn up something, we'll be leaving in a few days."

"I see." Raven turned her eyes toward Elizabeth. "If you'll leave me your measurements, I could make a dress for you and mail it to Atlanta."

"That would be wonderful, only—" she glanced from Michael to Ben and on to Raven—"I'm not sure about my measurements anymore. I'll have to send them by Ben, I suppose." Elizabeth realized Raven must have a tape measure so that she could get her measurements for the dress now, but she wanted Ben to have an excuse to come back.

"Yes, I can drop off the order at Raven's shop," Ben readily agreed.

They began walking from the kitchen across the living room. At the front door, Elizabeth turned back. She so wanted to leave the book of Psalms in her purse with Raven, but at the same time, she didn't want to seem intrusive. "I hope to see you again," she said, extending her hand to Raven. "Thank you so much for your hospitality."

"You are welcome," she said, looking directly into Elizabeth's eyes.

For a moment, Elizabeth felt something pricking at her, and she wondered if she should leave the book of Psalms anyway. She decided to wait.

"Well, good-bye," Michael said for both of them as he opened the front door.

As they left the cabin and headed back to the Blazer, Michael murmured, "I'm sure Ben was glad to see us go so he can have Raven all to himself."

Elizabeth nodded. "It bothers me that she's not a believer."

"Give her time. I think what we said about our faith may have more impact on her than she indicated. She seems to be a deep, thoughtful person."

"Yes, she does, doesn't she?"

They were back in the Blazer now, and Michael was turning the key in the ignition.

"Now what?" she asked.

"Now home to the chalet. I have some calls I want to make. There's still one angle in Knoxville I haven't explored."

"Sue Wilkens?"

He nodded. "She's the only one we haven't spoken with, and I think I need to follow up."

Elizabeth sighed. "I suppose so. But I just can't believe that woman would have anything to do with Mary's disappearance." Her thoughts turned to Katie as they drove home, and neither spoke for several miles. "I insist on calling Katie as soon as we get home."

"I agree," Michael said. "And tonight she'll still be up."

When they arrived at the chalet, Michael waited to return two phone calls until they had both chatted with Katie, who gave them a full running account of her activities at school and the fact that Granny had said Brooke could come spend the night on the weekend.

"You two just don't drive your grandmother crazy," Elizabeth teased.

"Oh, Mom!" Katie giggled.

When she hung up, Elizabeth looked at Michael. "I feel better, don't you?"

"I do. I'm so grateful for Katie. Well," he sighed, "back to work."

Two phone messages were taped to their door. One from Wyn, which was no surprise, and the other from Mrs. McCreary, who had left her home phone. Michael decided to call her first.

After polite greetings, Michael listened while Mrs. McCreary began to speak. "That's very helpful," he answered, looking across at Elizabeth. "I appreciate the call. No, we haven't made any progress, but maybe tomorrow....Thank you, Mrs. McCreary."

He hung up and looked across at Elizabeth.

"What is it?" she asked, instantly reading the concern on his face.

"Sue Wilkens's daughter has the same blood type as Mary Chamblis. B negative."

Elizabeth stared at him. "But...they wouldn't have had to kidnap Mary to get her blood, Michael. She'd gladly have donated it."

He nodded. "True. But would she have donated a kidney?"

THIRTEEN

"Would you like me to make some herbal tea?" Raven turned back to Ben as the sound of the Calloways's vehicle faded into the night.

"No, thank you. I ate so much of your chowder there's no room for anything else."

He was seated on the sofa, and she had taken the chair opposite him. Suddenly there was an awkward silence between them, and Ben cleared his throat and opened the conversation.

"I want to thank you for inviting us to eat, especially the Calloways. I could tell they really enjoyed themselves. This has been a difficult assignment for Michael. He's the kind of guy who hates to give up on something."

A faint smile touched her lips. "He sounds a bit like his employer, who appears determined to find the missing woman."

Ben shrugged, "Well, the employer may have to give it up. If she were in the area, I think Michael would have found her. I'm afraid she fell and—"

"Please." She put up her hand. "Could we talk about something else?"

"I'm sorry," Ben quickly replied. "I didn't mean to sound insensitive."

She shook her head, and the dark braid swung lightly. "You aren't insensitive. That story makes me sad."

Ben nodded. "Then let's discuss you. I hope you won't think I'm being too forward if I say you are one of the most fascinating people I've ever met."

Her eyes widened momentarily; then a tinge of color touched her cheeks. Ben noticed and felt as though he had again blundered. She was obviously a modest, shy woman, unaccustomed to someone's being so frank, particularly a stranger, which he was at this point.

"I think you are fascinated because of who I represent," she answered softly, folding her hands in her lap and studying her slim fingers thoughtfully.

"That's true, but it's more. You're gentle and thoughtful and sensitive. You're a pleasant change from some of the people I've known." He leaned forward, pressing his elbows on his legs, cupping his chin in his hands. "You seem so…at peace. How do you manage that?"

"At peace?" she repeated. She frowned slightly, lifting her eyes to study a beadwork design on the wall. "I was not at peace when I went away to school. I am more at peace here because it is the setting in which I have chosen to live, and I am living as I please."

He nodded. "I think that says a lot." He looked around the cabin. "I'm really impressed with the fact that you live so frugally and are happy doing so. Believe me, my sister would think she was on another planet if she was more than three blocks from a mall."

Raven nodded. "I understand. Many people seem to want that kind of lifestyle. It just happens that I don't."

Her eyes locked with his, and he felt his heart beating faster. What was happening to him? It was as though he had stepped into a magical world that he had only dreamed of, as far as his feelings were concerned. He wanted to understand those feelings better. Had she been right in her assessment of his fascination? Was she merely the embodiment of a people he admired greatly? He thought back to the first day he saw her, standing on her front porch of this quaint log cabin. Suddenly he was voicing those thoughts without thinking through his words.

"When I first saw you," he said quietly, "for a moment I thought—" He broke off, wondering if she would think he was being overly dramatic.

"You thought what?" she prompted, leaning forward, studying him intently.

He grinned and knew his expression probably displayed how foolish he felt. "I thought you were a vision, an angel," he laughed, trying to lighten such a bold statement. "I had been reading a book on angels, and I guess those thoughts were still on my mind."

"Oh? Tell me about what you read."

He leaned back on the sofa, stretching his arms across the back, forcing his thoughts back to the book. "The book was written by a minister who had done extensive research on angels. He used Scripture to support his belief in angels."

"Scripture from the Bible? What kind of Scripture?"

He crossed an ankle over his knee and stared at his hiking boots. "I remember one verse in particular. It was in Psalms. It said that God commands his angels to guard us in all our ways. I believe that angels are God's messengers sent into our lives to protect us during times of danger or to bring comfort or joy."

"You really believe that?" she asked, her face tilted in rapt interest. And before he could answer, she asked a more personal question. "And what am I?"

He held her gaze. "You are an angel of joy."

She did not answer; she merely stared at him. He forced himself to continue, hoping to edge toward something more general. "As to why I believe in angels, when I was a reckless sixteen-year-old, I was driving a mountain road during a blizzard. The road had been iced over, and my car started to slide on a curve. I was too inexperienced and terrified to know what to do. For a split second, I thought I saw a tall man standing on the edge of the drop-off where I was headed. To keep from hitting him, I steered back left, then right again. Even the car seemed to have lost its momentum, as though the man had, through brute strength, reached out and steadied it, and I ended up scrunched against the mountain wall. I got out on shaky knees, looking for the man to thank him. But…there was no one there. I walked and looked and called out. No one answered."

He looked at her and shook his head. "I never figured it out. My mom later told me she often prayed for guardian angels to keep me safe, and I must confess I needed them back in my teen years. So," he said, shrugging, "I just refer to that night as the time my guardian angel saved my life. Of course, some of my more skeptical friends said my so-called vision was induced by what I had to drink at the party that night. I don't think what happened was a vision brought on by one cup of punch, but I've never tried to convince anyone. And I don't often tell the story."

"I think it's a fascinating story," she said, her eyes wide. "And I believe you." She stared off into space for a moment, then looked back at him. "I had a friend in school who believed in ghosts, but, of course, that's not the same as angels."

Ben shook his head. "Not at all. Or at least not to my way of thinking. I don't believe in ghosts, but I believe in angels."

She leaned back in her chair and studied him thoughtfully. "Some of my people believe in spirits that live here in the mountains and guard us. They say that spirits live in the mists, that when we look out on the fog that often shrouds the mountains that the spirits dwell there."

Ben was silent for a moment, wondering how he should

respond. He decided he might as well be truthful. "My personal belief," he said gently, "is that there is only one spirit, the Holy Spirit."

Raven was silent, obviously thinking that over. "Maybe I should learn more about the Christian religion. For a long time I rejected it, but after meeting you and the Calloways, I am interested. You are kind and caring people; you are *real*, and I like that. I have known many people who are one way on the outside but quite different on the inside. That has been disillusioning for me. But I shouldn't have judged all Christians by the few who did not live up to their religious values."

"That's right. And after all, nobody is perfect." He realized he now had the opening he had been waiting for. "If you wouldn't mind, I'd like to bring you some books on Christianity. Maybe even a Bible, if that's okay."

She nodded. "I would like that."

Their eyes locked for a moment, and Ben realized that it was getting harder for him to hide his feelings for this woman. In fact, he needed to be alone to sort through what was going on in his head. He realized he was on the brink of falling in love, and he hardly knew her. He had to spend more time with her, get to know her better. He forced himself to his feet, glancing at his watch.

"I have an early appointment, so I guess I'd better go."

She stood, crossing her arms. "I enjoyed our conversation."

"So did I." Then he surprised himself again. "Could I take you to dinner one night? Any night you're free?"

When she hesitated, he plunged on.

"Hey, it's the least I can do to repay you for the corn chowder."

"All right," she said slowly. "I'm free on Friday evening."

"Friday evening will be perfect. I'll bring Elizabeth's order at that time, if you like."

She nodded. "Sure."

She turned and walked toward the door, and he followed. As she opened the door, the soft darkness drifted over the front porch, illuminated by a three-quarter moon. Glancing back at her, he saw that her eyes were dark like the night, and yet they reflected the silver glow of the moon. She was so fragile and perfect, and still there was something about her that warned him to keep his distance. Ben fought a desire to kiss her, instinctively knowing that with this woman he had to move slowly, very slowly. Or, like the shy creatures in the surrounding woods, she would quickly slip away.

"Good night, Raven," he said, forcing himself to step onto the porch.

"Good night," she said.

By the time he reached the steps, she had already closed the door. Breathing the sweetness of the crisp air, he lengthened his steps and reached the truck. Once he had opened the door and hopped in, he cast a glance, one longing glance, toward the cabin, and saw her there, framed in the window. With a lamp as backlight, her silhouette was perfectly framed in the square window. Once again he found himself thinking of angels.

FOURTEEN

The next morning Michael and Elizabeth were on their way to Knoxville to check into Sue Wilkens's background.

"What are you going to say to her?" Elizabeth asked. She had prayed that Sue was not involved in any way in what had happened to Mary. But who was left?

"I don't know." Michael shook his head. "But first I want to speak with Wyn. I think it's only appropriate that I voice my suspicions to him first. After all, the woman seems to be well respected by everyone in her department."

Elizabeth nodded, looking out the window. It was a beautiful autumn day, with the soft golden light of late September spreading over the valleys and hillsides. Elizabeth knew she would miss the special beauty here, but she was homesick to go back to Oak Shadows now. She had prayed earnestly last night that Michael would locate Mary, or that someone, anyone, would find her. It was beginning to seem hopeless.

She looked across at Michael, deep in thought. "Do you suppose Charlie made it into that rehab center in Nashville?"

"We'll find out today," he said, frowning. "You know, Elizabeth, maybe I'm trusting my instincts too much and not relying on facts the way I should."

"Then let's discuss the facts."

"Okay." Michael leaned back against the car seat, his arm draped over the steering wheel and thought for a moment. "Who has a motive for Mary's disappearance?"

"And what was the motive?" Elizabeth prompted, getting accustomed to the way Michael approached his cases.

"The motive had to be money. What else was at stake here?"

Elizabeth nodded. "So if money is the motive, who has the strongest one?"

They were silent for a moment. Then Elizabeth sighed. "Sue Wilkens."

When Michael had returned Wyn's call the previous evening, they had set up an appointment for ten o'clock. As Michael wheeled into the parking lot, he noted they only had five minutes to spare.

He and Elizabeth hurried up to the complex of corporate offices, and Wyn's secretary ushered them right through the door. "He's expecting you," the older woman said, giving them a brief smile. She was the epitome of dignity and reserve, just the right kind of secretary for Wyn Dalton, Elizabeth decided.

"Good morning." Wyn greeted them with a pleasant smile.

Elizabeth smiled back, relieved that he was in a better frame of mind than yesterday, when he had barreled up to their chalet, hoping Mary had been found, and was so bitterly disappointed that he had taken out his ire on them.

"Morning," Michael said, nodding acceptance at the coffee that was offered.

"No, thank you," Elizabeth said, wondering if either man needed more caffeine.

Wyn returned to his chair behind the desk, and Michael and Elizabeth took their seats across from him. "I want to apologize for being abrupt yesterday," Wyn said, looking embarrassed. "I was just so frustrated over Mary."

"We understand," Michael said and nodded. Yet Elizabeth

noticed that her husband sounded more formal with his employer today.

"I want to discuss Sue Wilkens with you," Michael said, coming right to the point.

"Sue Wilkens?" Wyn put down his coffee cup and leaned forward. "Did you find out something about her?"

"Her daughter who needs the kidney transplant has the same blood type as Mary."

Wyn stared for a moment; then he began to shake his head. "Sue wouldn't have been involved in anything like this. She has no motive."

"What about thirty thousand dollars?" Michael asked, not venturing any further with his suspicions.

"Not even that. I learned this morning that the fund that was started for Sue's daughter has now achieved its goal. Thirty-two thousand, to be exact, has been raised; and the transplant is scheduled for tomorrow."

Michael sat back in his seat, staring at Wyn. "So do you think that rules out any suspicions against Sue?"

"I do. And besides," he added, shaking his head, "I tend to be suspicious, but I can tell you for sure that Sue Wilkens would have no part of anything like that. So where does that leave us?" He looked squarely at Michael.

"It leads us back to Charlie."

"Virginia called just before you arrived to say that her son is now in a rehab clinic in Nashville."

"I have my doubts about Charlie's being involved, but I don't know anything about the crowd he runs around with, particularly if it's a drug crowd. From my experience, they'll do anything for money."

Wyn nodded. "That possibility seems to make more sense than any others we've considered. Anyone else?"

Michael's eyes drifted over Wyn's face. "I still have the key to Mary's apartment. I'd like your permission to go through it one more time."

Wyn's eyebrows arched. "Sure. But what do you hope to find?"

Michael stroked his chin. "I'm not sure. I guess I just want to be sure I've covered all the bases before I throw in the towel. You said give it a couple more days; tomorrow is the last day."

Wyn hesitated. "If you're onto something, of course I want you to continue working for me. And I think Charlie's friends might be the best place to look. You're sure she isn't around Angel Valley or any of those remote areas?"

"The posters are everywhere, Wyn. With the enticing reward you're offering, I think someone would have come forward."

Wyn nodded, staring at his desk.

Michael drained his coffee mug and came to his feet. "I'll check in with you later today. After we go through Mary's apartment, I'm going back to see Charlie's girlfriend to find out more about his friends."

"All right; just keep me informed," he said, coming to his feet.

Michael nodded, taking Elizabeth's arm.

"Good-bye," she said and smiled at Wyn.

He looked from her to Michael, a sadness passing over his features. "Good-bye."

After they were back on the elevator, Elizabeth turned to Michael. "Did you notice the way he looked at us when we were leaving? Almost as though he envied us."

Michael nodded, looking down at Elizabeth. "He probably does."

"So are we going straight to Mary's apartment, or are you going to question Virginia Redgrave again?"

Michael shook his head. "No. Virginia doesn't have the answers. If she did, she wouldn't give them to us."

Elizabeth nodded. "All she did was cast suspicion upon her employer."

As she spoke the words, her eyes drifted across to Michael. He was staring thoughtfully at the floor. "What do you think of Wyn Dalton?" she asked as the elevator doors slid open.

"I'll answer that question later," he said under his breath as they walked swiftly past the receptionist's eagle eye.

"Well, what do you think of Wyn Dalton?" Elizabeth repeated the question as they drove toward Mary's apartment.

"I wish you hadn't asked."

Elizabeth tilted her head back in surprise. "Why do you say that? I mean, I find him a bit pushy, but I thought that was just the female in me. What is it with you?"

"I'm not sure. You know I just made the statement earlier that I had to stick to facts and quit relying on my intuition since it's getting me nowhere."

"Just for the sake of argument, what does your intuition tell you about Wyn?"

Michael braked the Blazer, waiting for a red light to turn. "I think he's a very controlling man. Remember what Virginia told us?"

Elizabeth nodded. "Even Claire admitted that Mary was a passive kind of person, and the fact that she was indebted to the family made the situation worse."

"That missing twenty thousand still bothers me, and the fact that Mary seemed preoccupied with it makes me even more suspicious."

"Of what?" Her brown eyes widened as she studied her husband's slim profile. "You aren't suggesting that Mary took the money and ran out, are you?"

"I must admit the thought has occurred to me. It's the reason I want to go back to her apartment."

Elizabeth shook her head. "From everything we've heard about her, she just wouldn't abscond with funds from a family who had been so good to her."

"Nobody seems capable of doing this deed, but somebody did. We can't forget that for a second."

Elizabeth stared absently at the traffic as Michael turned down the side street leading to Mary's condo. "If money is the motive, the one person we shouldn't suspect is Wyn, and here we've just been talking about him as though...," her voice trailed. "Listen Michael, just for the sake of argument, what if Virginia's speculation was correct? They got into an argument, he lost his temper, maybe shoved her, and she accidentally fell over a ledge?"

Michael hit the steering wheel with his fist. "Why hasn't her body been found?"

"Maybe..." Elizabeth's eyes grew wider as they pulled into the parking lot of Mary's condominium complex. "Michael, that's it! Maybe Wyn hired you to be sure Mary's body had not been overlooked."

Michael nodded, cutting the engine. "You're getting to be a very good detective, Elizabeth." He reached across and kissed her lips. "The problem is, why hasn't she been found?"

Elizabeth was puzzled. "I don't know."

They got out of the Blazer and hurried up to Mary's condo. Elizabeth felt less intrusive this time as Michael unlocked the door and they entered the quiet foyer.

"This time we're really going to take the place apart," Michael said.

"What?" Elizabeth whirled, surprised. "What are we looking for?"

"A checkbook, a deposit slip, banking records."

"You still think she might have taken the money?"

"I'm not ruling it out. And we're looking for anything that might incriminate Wyn. Don't ask me what that would be—I don't know."

"Bloodstains," Elizabeth gasped as the knowledge hit her. "We only have his word that they went to the mountains together, that she disappeared when he went into the men's room."

"Nope, there's a flaw in that theory too."

"What's the flaw?" Elizabeth asked, wondering if she was a good detective, after all. What had she missed?

"Remember the Fishers in Birmingham? They said they saw Wyn and Mary drive up together as they were leaving."

"Oh." Elizabeth's breath swooshed out of her chest in a huge sigh of disappointment. "The Fishers. Do you think—?"

"Nope. No motive. And I trust Jay's instincts."

"Then maybe we need to get Jay up here working on this case, because our instincts aren't paying off."

He winked at her. "Don't give up so quickly. Come on. We have a condo to search."

An hour later, after going through every drawer and every cabinet, there was no evidence that Mary had absconded with the money. Her bank statements were neatly stacked in the desk drawer, along with her deposit records showing a balance of three thousand, three hundred and twenty-seven dollars.

"Not enough for an elaborate wedding," Elizabeth said, looking thoughtful.

"Come on. You know Wyn's family was picking up the tab for the wedding. Mary was probably paying for her dress and her honeymoon stuff, or whatever it is you ladies buy."

"It's called a trousseau." Elizabeth wrinkled her nose at him as she wandered back into the kitchen and poked around one more time. She opened the cabinet drawers and peered inside. "Not much silverware. Not even a can opener!" she said, looking at Michael. "The woman never even opened a can."

"Why should she when they dined out every night?"

Elizabeth shook her head. "Everybody has a can opener, which reminds me that I'm getting hungry. What about you?"

Michael nodded. "In a minute." His eyes skimmed over the kitchen, taking in every detail. Then he walked back into the living room and stood with his hands on his hips, taking in the ultramodern furnishings.

"Elizabeth, you said you checked out her wardrobe? Nothing's missing?"

"Looks as though she was planning to go to work on Monday as always. Every name-brand suit was properly hung; there were plenty of frilly underthings and lacy gowns." She frowned, turning back to the bedroom. "Let me check again."

She went in and sat down on the bed, letting her eyes move slowly over the room. It was in perfect order, with the exception of some dainty pink house shoes peering from under the bed. She walked over and opened the dresser drawers again. The jewelry box held some impressive pieces, so if robbery was a motive, why hadn't someone grabbed her key and taken the jewelry? She saw something wrapped in tissue paper and unfolded it. There was a beaded necklace very similar to the one Elizabeth had bought.

"I agree with her taste on one item," she said, recalling that Laurel Wentworth had said she liked to shop for native arts and crafts.

She closed the drawer and opened the remaining ones, finding nothing out of order. She turned to the chest of drawers and opened each one. The top one held an assortment of frilly underwear. The second one held only a few casual T-shirts; the third drawer was empty. She frowned at that, opening the bottom drawer. Three very silky nightgowns, still bearing the price tags were neatly folded. Elizabeth opened the empty drawer again. What had been in that drawer? Was it something Wyn Dalton had come back to remove?

She went over to the closet and opened the doors again, peering in at the way everything was arranged. It was almost...too perfect, she decided. She checked the hangers again, frowning. There was that nagging doubt again, something she couldn't quite pinpoint. She stared at the shoes, mostly high heels, half a dozen loafers and casual shoes. No hiking boots or tennis shoes. She was wearing jeans, a white sweater, and a pair of tennis shoes when she disappeared, Wyn had said. That explained the absence of tennis shoes. She closed the door.

Returning to the living room, she threw up her hands. "One empty drawer. Does that mean anything?"

He shook his head. "Not if everything else is in place. Wait a minute. Is it a drawer that would contain business items?"

"Nope. Lacy underwear and very sleek gowns for her honeymoon." She lifted her eyebrows and blinked coquettishly at Michael.

"As sleek as yours were?"

"Much sleeker," she laughed. "You know me—plain Jane."

"My darling, nothing about you is plain. As for the empty drawer, maybe Mary had already started taking a few things over to Wyn's place. We could ask him."

"Yeah." Elizabeth cast one last glance over the room. She walked over and picked up the picture of Wyn and Mary. The golden sheen of Mary's hair set her apart from the everyday woman. It would be hard to miss that hair if someone were looking for a body. She quickly replaced the picture, not wanting to pursue those thoughts.

Michael was staring at the picture of Mary's parents. "She must look like her father, with the fair coloring and all."

Elizabeth studied the picture, her forehead rumpling slightly. What was it…?

Michael sighed. "Well, shall we admit to another strikeout and head to Sevierville to see what we can dig up on Charlie's friends?"

Elizabeth threw her hands up. "That seems to be the last alternative."

This time they located Betsy at her apartment, and Elizabeth liked her immediately. She was a pretty young woman with short auburn hair and green gray eyes. She was friendly and polite, inviting them inside. This time the apartment was pleasantly clean, and things were in order.

Michael looked around. "Where's your roommate?"

Betsy sighed. "She's no longer my roommate. I don't know what kind of miracle you two worked when you came here, but Sandy was crying and packing when I returned, and Charlie was waiting for me to take him to the rehab clinic in Nashville." She looked from Elizabeth to Michael. "I can't thank you enough for pushing him to do this. Charlie's a great guy. He just needs to get well. I don't do drugs," she said emphatically. "I'm going to school to be a nurse, and I'm very opposed to abusing the body. I'm working my way through college, so Mr. Farley at the linen outlet allows me to work around my school schedule."

"Oh, that's nice." Elizabeth smiled at her.

"And I want to thank you two for leaving the little book of

Psalms. Do you know that Charlie was actually reading it when I came home that day? And Sandy…" She shook her head, dropping her eyes. "Well, she apologized to me for being such a lousy person. She never said exactly what she had done, but Charlie told me on the way to Nashville."

"You're a very forgiving young lady," Michael said.

"I'm a Christian," she said, her eyes glowing. "I know the power of forgiveness. I was almost as messed up as Charlie. Then Mom got me back in church, and I turned my life around. I believe God is working in this, that Charlie will really get straightened out this time."

Michael and Elizabeth were listening to her and watching her face, which glowed with the kind of inner beauty that comes straight from the soul.

"Betsy, Charlie is a very lucky young man to have you in his life," Michael said.

"And keep praying for him," Elizabeth said and touched her hand. "I believe this time he's learned his lesson."

Betsy nodded; then suddenly her eyes were troubled. "You don't still think he might have had something to do with the disappearance of that prominent Knoxville woman, do you? I mean, why would anyone think that? Charlie is very tender-hearted. Even when he's high, he's always kind." She sighed. "I guess that's why I never gave up on him."

Michael nodded. "We're more suspicious of any of his companions. His mother said some of the crowd he ran with was pretty rough."

"Oh." The light of comprehension dawned in Betsy's eyes. "That much is true, but Charlie hasn't been seeing any of those guys since we got back together."

"When was that?" Michael inquired.

"Back in July. It was one of the rules I laid down when I

agreed to go back to him. If he wanted to see me again, he would have to give up those hoods in Knoxville."

"And you think he did?" Elizabeth asked gently.

"Oh, I know he did. We ran into one of them back in August, and Charlie wouldn't have anything to do with him. The guy said something about the old gang missing him. Even thinking about those guys—" she shook her head—"they're too messed up to pull off something as sophisticated as abducting Mary Chamblis. The newspaper said Mr. Dalton was with her. How could those guys have pulled something like that?" She shook her head. "I honestly don't think they had anything to do with it, but I'll be glad to get their names and phone numbers for you. I can call one of Charlie's friends and find out."

"I'd appreciate that, Betsy. We can't overlook anything." He handed her a business card with the telephone number of the chalet inked in. "Think you could check it out and give me a call tonight?"

"I'll be glad to," she replied. "I certainly hope you find her. Charlie said his mother really liked Mary, that everyone did."

"Which makes it all the more puzzling," Elizabeth said, as they turned to go.

"Do you have my phone number?" Betsy offered, then grinned. "I guess you do. You're a detective, right?"

They laughed and said good-bye after Betsy again promised to get the names and telephone numbers and call Michael right away.

As they headed back to their Blazer, Elizabeth looked up at Michael. "Well, what do you think now?"

"I think we just took the third strike and the game is about over."

222

When they walked in the door of the chalet, the telephone was ringing.

"Betsy works fast," Elizabeth laughed.

To their surprise, it was not Betsy but Jay on the other end of the line.

"Hey, brother," Michael said with a grin. "We were just talking about you earlier. No, it wasn't all bad. What Elizabeth said was that she wished you were here to share your instincts about this case."

Michael hesitated, glanced at Elizabeth, and arched his brows. "You may be right. Elizabeth and I discussed that possibility this morning. Thanks. Talk to you again soon. Give Tracie and little Brooke a hug."

After he hung up, he stared into space for a minute.

"What?" Elizabeth asked impatiently, tugging at his sleeve. "Come on, I'm codetective here, remember?"

"He called to say he had followed up on the couple in Birmingham, the Fishers. They still insist that they saw Wyn and Mary drive up and get out of their vehicle just as the Fishers were leaving. Jay's been digging to see if there's anything against these people, and there just isn't. Apparently they're just good, hardworking people who came up to enjoy a weekend in the Smokies and happened to spot Wyn and Mary."

"*Happened* to?" Elizabeth said, narrowing her eyes. "Do you realize that without their word, we have no proof that Mary and Wyn were together at Painted Rock that morning?"

"You're forgetting about the people he questioned on the trail and the fact that he went straight to the sheriff."

She nodded. "Which is exactly what he would do if he were

trying to cover his own tracks," Elizabeth said, biting the inside corner of her lip.

"You're getting good, babe; I'll have to admit it."

"I am?" She was enormously pleased.

"Yep. Your observation matches Jay's theory."

Elizabeth perked up. "Is that what Jay thinks?"

"He reminded me of the statistics on cases like this. When there's no where else to look, it's time to take another look at the source. In this case, the source is Wyn Dalton."

"Wait a minute, Michael." Elizabeth sank down on the sofa, her thoughts spinning. "These people, the Fishers, may be good, hardworking people, but we also know they're short on money. Do you think it's possible that Wyn paid them to say his girl-friend was with him? Otherwise, it's just his word to substantiate what happened."

Michael considered her words, taking a seat beside her. "And the whole thing could have been a setup. He and Mary could have argued—maybe at his place, not hers. Maybe he lost his temper; maybe there was an accident that he didn't want to report. So he gets in the car and drives up to the mountains and stages this disappearance. Is that what you're saying?"

She whirled to him, her eyes dancing. "Yes. That's my theory."

Michael frowned. "But Jay is convinced the Fishers are telling the truth."

"Then maybe Wyn paid off the Fishers." Elizabeth sighed.

"It's worth considering, Elizabeth."

The sound of an engine in the driveway broke through their thoughts. Michael looked through the sliding glass doors. "It's Ben," he said, coming to his feet.

"I'll get us something to drink," Elizabeth offered. They had stopped for lunch as they left Knoxville, but all the talking had left her with a dry throat.

"Hey, Michael," Ben called from the porch.

"Ben, come in. Elizabeth is getting—what?" He glanced toward the kitchen.

"Iced tea okay?"

"Sounds great." Ben grinned, as affable as ever.

"Well." Michael looked him over. "How are things with you?"

"Just great. I'm on my way to Raven's place, and I thought I'd take along Elizabeth's measurements for the dress."

Michael tapped his shoulder. "You'll do anything to get to see Raven, won't you?"

Ben nodded. "We talked for hours after you two left. When Michael and I first met her, she told us her parents were dead, and yet she's carried on the tradition of that family. Even though she went out to school for a while, she never forgot her roots. Said her heart was always back at that log cabin. She really is an incredible woman."

Elizabeth was smiling at Ben as she handed him a glass of tea, then set hers and Michael's down on the coffee table and nestled beside Michael on the sofa.

"Well, Ben," Michael said with a grin, "does she know you're falling in love with her?"

Ben looked startled, and for a moment Elizabeth thought he was actually going to blush. He grinned and took a sip of tea. Then he looked from Michael to Elizabeth. "She probably does."

"Hmm…" Michael looked at Elizabeth. "He's admitting it This is serious."

Elizabeth sipped her tea, saying nothing, looking very thoughtful. "Michael, let's take a break and ride over to Raven's place. We'll go in separate vehicles, Ben, and we won't stay long. But I want to pay her for the dress and leave my mailing address."

Ben shrugged. "Okay, if you want to."

"We can't stay long," Michael warned, "because Betsy will be calling us with those names, remember?"

"I know. We won't need to stay long, will we, Ben?"

"It's up to you," he said, rather smugly, as he sipped his tea.

"Ben, you're a believer, aren't you?" Elizabeth leaned forward.

"Yes, I am. I was raised in a Christian home, and while I admit to being a bit of a backslider, I do believe. And I have a Bible among my scattered possessions."

"Then why don't you loan it to Raven?" Elizabeth suggested gently.

He grinned. "As a matter of fact, I offered to bring her a Bible and some Christian books, but I don't want to push her."

"You don't have to push her," Michael said, "but just remember, if you're falling in love with her, your faith will be an important issue in this relationship."

"Right."

Elizabeth set down her tea glass. "Come on, guys. We're wasting time. You'll have lots of phone calls to make tonight, Michael; we'd better get going."

Within the hour they were knocking on Raven's door. Her smile was more trusting this time, particularly after Ben explained that they were returning to Atlanta and wanted to say good-bye.

She was wearing jeans and another sweatshirt, socks and Reeboks, and her hair was pulled back in a ponytail. The swirl of dark hair across her forehead accented her brown eyes. She wore no makeup, and yet she was so much prettier than someone like Mary Chamblis, with bleached hair and heavy makeup, Elizabeth concluded.

"Come in," Raven said, opening the door wider.

"Hi, Raven." Michael smiled.

"I used the dress as an excuse to see you before we left," Elizabeth said. "And to be honest, I'm too vain to be passing along my measurements. After giving birth to a nine-pound baby girl, my waist never returned to normal," she said, laughing.

"You don't seem vain at all," Raven said, looking at her with admiration. "And, believe me, I know the difference."

"You do?" Elizabeth asked, as they followed her into the living room and took a seat.

"Yes. I've met women in the city. Would you like to go into my bedroom where I have a tape measure, and we can get your measurements there?"

"Raven, may I show Michael the beadwork you've just begun? It's really incredible," Ben was saying to Michael.

"Yes, it's there on the sewing machine."

"I never had the patience for sewing," Elizabeth said, following Raven into her small bedroom.

"I find it very relaxing," Raven said, crossing the bedroom to her dresser, where the tape measure was neatly coiled. "Please excuse the state of my bedroom. I've been absorbed in my beadwork today."

Elizabeth nodded, staring at Raven's dresser, where half a dozen pairs of socks were neatly folded.

"Socks," Elizabeth said, staring at the simple white cotton socks. "That's what was missing."

Raven dropped the tape measure at Elizabeth's outburst. She bent to pick it up. "I beg your pardon?"

"We went to Mary's condo and looked around. I couldn't pinpoint what was missing from the empty drawer, but now I know. There were no socks anywhere in the bedroom."

Raven stared at Elizabeth as though she were half crazy.

"Sorry, I know that doesn't make sense," Elizabeth said quickly, "but you see…"

"What is it?" Raven asked, looking curiously at Elizabeth.

"Oh, I'm sorry. I didn't mean to stare. But I was just wondering.…"

Raven turned her back, reaching for a small notepad and pen. "Yes?"

Elizabeth's eyes ran up and down her slim body, lingering on the glossy dark ponytail.

"I was wondering about the beadwork you do."

Raven turned around, looking relieved that Elizabeth was finally making sense again. "Yes, what about it? Hold your arms straight out and let me measure from your shoulders to your wrist," Raven instructed.

Elizabeth obeyed, her thoughts in a whirl now. "Raven, if I asked you a question, you'd give me an honest answer, wouldn't you? What I mean is, you seem like a very straightforward person, someone who wouldn't lie."

"I don't lie." Raven's dark eyes met Elizabeth's, then dropped to the tape measure as she noted the length of Elizabeth's arm and made a notation on the pad.

"Do you know Mary Chamblis?" Elizabeth asked.

Raven's eyes shot to Elizabeth's face. "I told your husband that first day that Mary Chamblis did not come here."

Elizabeth nodded. "I know. But that's not what I asked you. I asked if you know her."

Raven took a deep breath and released it slowly. She laid the tape measure on the dresser beside the pad and pen. "Yes," she answered.

Elizabeth nodded. "I thought so. I saw a necklace in her drawer, very much like the one I bought from you. The beadwork is exquisite, better than the others in Cherokee or Angel Valley."

Raven sighed, staring into space. "The women in my family were gifted with beadwork and sewing. My mother taught me how when I was very young. I suppose my work is a bit different."

"So at some point, you sold Mary Chamblis a necklace?"

Raven hesitated, dropping her eyes.

"I don't want to ask you to betray a confidence. Surely you understand that everyone who cares about Mary is worried sick. We're merely trying to help. I sense you're hiding something; perhaps you even know where Mary is."

Slowly Raven's eyes lifted to meet Elizabeth's concerned gaze.

"I can't explain what it is," Elizabeth said, looking from the socks to Raven's eyes, "but somehow I see—no, I feel—there is a connection between you and Mary."

Raven took a deep breath and leaned back, gripping the dresser with both hands. "Yes, there is a connection. I am Mary Chamblis."

FIFTEEN

Feeling both amused and happy for his friend, Michael studied Ben carefully as they sat in the living room of Raven's small cabin. Ben's eyes were glowing, and his voice swelled with pride as he spoke of Raven's talent. "I think she needs to open her own shop," he was saying when the bedroom door opened and both women returned to the living room.

One look at Elizabeth made Michael's eyes widen. Her cheeks were flushed, and her eyes were virtually snapping with some news. He looked at Raven. There were tears forming in her dark eyes as she walked over to stand beside Ben.

"There is something I must tell you," she said to Ben.

Elizabeth tugged at Michael's hand, pulling him down on the sofa with her. He gave her a what's-going-on look and she nodded toward Raven. *Just listen.* She mouthed the words as Raven shyly took Ben's hand.

"You've been so kind and caring. I've never known anyone quite like you," Raven said to Ben.

Ben's eyes lit up, and a smile zipped over his face. He glanced nervously at Michael and Elizabeth. "Why, thank you. I feel the same way about you."

"You might not," she said, releasing his hand, "when you hear what I have to say."

Elizabeth squeezed Michael's hand. He couldn't possibly imagine what was going on, or why Elizabeth looked as though she were about to come out of her skin.

"Nothing you say will change my feelings for you, Raven," he said emphatically.

"What if I told you I have another name? That Raven is the name my mother lovingly called me, and then my father as well. But my other name is Mary. Mary Chamblis."

Michael gasped so loudly Elizabeth thought he might choke. Ben, on the other hand, froze in his tracks, never moving a muscle as he took in this astounding announcement. Then his eyes began to sweep over her face, her hair, her clothing.

"But...but you look nothing like her."

"No, I look like who I really am. A Native American who loves the mountains and my people. Mary Chamblis was a victim of circumstances. Her parents had to leave here so her father ould find work in the city. At the time, the reservation was not thriving as it is today. Dad got a job with Dalton Chemicals when I was a little girl. I grew up thinking the Daltons were royalty, and yet it broke my mother's heart to see her daughter straying so far from who she really was. You see, the Daltons did not want to acknowledge that I am Cherokee. They couldn't stop Wyn's obsession with me, so they had to make me acceptable for their world."

She took a deep breath and walked over to sit down on a stool. "After my mother's automobile accident, Wyn's father helped Dad handle the expense of lawyers in the lawsuit filed against my mother. Then while she was ill, they saw to it that she had the best medical care possible until her death. My father was very indebted to them, but he and I slipped away at least once a month to come back here. I never told Wyn about the cabin. It was my own special place, and I felt he didn't belong here."

Her eyes roamed over the room, as though mentally touching each object. "My father made every item of furniture that you see; it was a labor of love. He and Mother and I came often when I was a child, but then after the car accident and her illness, we rarely came. Later, to help my father through his depression, I suggested that we start coming back here again. He hoped to live here when he retired."

The tears Raven had held at bay now trickled down her cheeks. "But one day he was vital and strong, and the next day, he had a massive heart attack and died. I missed him terribly. Wyn took advantage of my vulnerability, and finally the Daltons realized it was no use. Wyn was determined to have me. The problem was——" she looked at the three of them through a sheen of tears—"what he wanted was a woman he could manufacture like their chemicals. He had this image of a striking blond with polish and sophistication, so that's who I became." She lifted a strand of her hair. "My hair is a medium brown. I had it professionally bleached and my brows lightened. My nervousness destroyed my appetite, and I had become very thin, but he liked me that way. I let him select a condo and most of the furnishings, even my clothes. Then there was no more Raven, just a cardboard Mary Chamblis."

Ben had finally found his voice. "Did you...love Wyn?"

She shook her head. "No. But I was grateful to him and his family for all they had done for my parents and for me. I thought I could grow to love him, that I could eventually fit into their social world, and I tried. But then I became more and more miserable. Whenever I said or did anything that displeased Wyn, he lost his temper and made me feel ungrateful and immature."

She folded her hands in her lap and studied her slim fingers. "I knew I couldn't live like that for the rest of my life, even though he continued with our wedding plans. I began to bring only the items that were really *me* to this cabin—the clothes I preferred to wear, the treasures I wanted to keep. I don't know if I would have actually gone through with my disappearance, however, if not for Wyn."

She looked directly at Michael. "Wyn made a trip to Las Vegas with some of his bachelor friends, and he lost money, way too much money. He took the money out of the company, with plans to pay it back, but I caught the mistake. That last week, I knew I could not marry this kind of man, that no matter what I owed his family, I owed *him* nothing, after all. We had planned a drive up to the mountains on Saturday. I wanted a private place for us to talk. I had hoped to convince him to balance the books, to sell some of his possessions. When we got out at Painted Rock, it was quiet and peaceful, and I felt my courage returning, because I was becoming the real me again.

"When I confronted him, he was furious. He said some awful things to me. I gave back his engagement ring, and he struck me."

Ben was muttering something from a corner of the room, but Michael motioned to him to keep quiet until she had finished her story.

"I fell down the trail, not over the rock, as some people think. Of course, he thought I would get up and come back to him and say I was sorry. Instead, I slipped deeper into the woods and hid from him. When he didn't find me on that trail, he took another one. I ran through the woods then." She looked at Ben. "I used the same route that you and Michael took, only nobody had followed it that far. I knew about the back country from tagging after my father. It took hours to get to the cabin, but once I came in here and closed the door, I felt a kind of freedom I had never known in my life."

"But your hair...?" Ben was gaping at her, still trying to absorb all he had heard.

"I wore it in a long bob when I ran away. I simply brushed it out straight and dyed my hair and my brows." She sighed.

"It was a game in the beginning, dreaming about running away from Wyn, coming here to start a new life, doing the kind of work that had always interested me. I hated accounting and stenographic work; I only took those courses to assure my father that I could make a living for myself if necessary. I had been unable to eat for weeks, but suddenly my appetite returned. When I got here, all I wanted to do was eat, and within two weeks I had gained seven pounds. I styled my hair like that of my grandmother, and I was perfectly content to live a simple life here. I've never missed the glamour of the city, the fine restaurants where Wyn threw money around every night, or the ugly modern condo that he forced on me."

She paused, taking a long deep breath. "I never want to go back to that other life, and I hope that by telling you the truth, I will finally be completely free."

No one spoke for several seconds. Then Michael looked at Elizabeth. "You suspected something; you picked up on something I missed."

She smiled. "Today I realized there was some connection between Raven and Mary. Remember the empty drawer at the condo? I couldn't think what was missing in a woman's wardrobe until I saw the socks on Raven's dresser. There were no socks in Mary's bedroom anywhere. Every woman has at least one pair of socks. And it bugged me that there was no can opener, that always seemed odd."

"The can opener and some cutlery were the first items I brought, along with my favorite jeans and sweatshirts. I never did get the picture of my parents," Raven sighed. "That has always made me sad."

That's the other thing." Elizabeth nodded slowly, looking at

Michael. "Remember her mother? The woman in the picture had a high forehead, dark hair, and eyes the color of Raven's eyes. Raven covers her forehead with bangs, but when we were in the bedroom and I was close to Raven, I recognized the resemblance to her mother. I suspected Raven could be Mary. But I wasn't sure until she admitted it to me."

Ben crossed the room and extended his hand to Raven. Shyly she placed her hand in his, and he gently pulled her up from the stool and wrapped her lovingly in his arms. "I'm so sorry for all you've been through. But I'm so glad we've met, that you returned to your roots, that you became who you really are, for that is the person I love."

Michael and Elizabeth exchanged a swift glance. Michael stood up, pulling Elizabeth with him. "I think you two need to have some time alone to talk."

Raven looked across at him, her dark eyes turning sad again. "What are you going to do? You'll tell Wyn, of course."

"The first thing that needs to be done is for you to get a restraining order against him, but it probably won't be necessary."

"No," Ben said, clearly angry. "He'd better not come near her."

"I don't think he'll want to, Ben. I think if Raven agrees to live her life and let him live his, he should be more than happy not to be charged with extorting funds from the corporation. After all, it is a corporation with stockholders and other family members. If he will agree to quietly return the money, perhaps Raven will assure him that she won't press charges against his physical abuse at Painted Rock. Unless you want to." Michael looked at her.

She shook her head. "It was the best thing he's ever done for me. At last he gave me the incentive I needed to leave him, to leave behind all that I hated and come home. And this is really home. So, no, I won't press charges against him if he will agree to stay out of my life. Forever."

Elizabeth could no longer restrain herself. She walked over to touch Raven's hand. "I admire you so much. It took a lot of courage to survive all that you have."

"Sometimes I don't feel that I have survived it very well. At night, especially, I feel empty and alone and...tormented."

"In that case—" Elizabeth glanced at Michael and smiled, then turned back to Raven—"maybe sometime we can talk more about faith, the kind of faith that has kept Michael and me so strong. A faith that Ben embraces as well."

Raven looked from Elizabeth to Ben. "You don't believe in the spirit world, do you?"

Ben shook his head. "Not the way you do."

"Raven, there's only one true spirit in our faith," Michael said gently. "The Holy Spirit. God was with you that day at Painted Rock, whether you felt his presence or not."

"I did," she said quietly. "When I made that long, tortuous trip, I knew I was not alone. But I thought perhaps it was the spirits of my parents calling me home to the cabin."

"I'm sure you felt their love as well; but you see, God holds on to us even when we don't care about him. He holds on, and he never gives up. Don't you think he's sent Ben into your life?"

Raven nodded, looking tenderly at Ben.

"And the funny thing was—" Ben smiled into her eyes— "the day Michael and I came out of the woods onto the trail and I saw you on the porch, I thought I was having a vision. That you were some kind of special angel. And you are."

"Well, we'll go now," Michael said. "I'll meet with Wyn Dalton first thing in the morning, and then I'll call Ben." He looked around. "Since you don't have a phone. Ben can relay the news to you."

Raven closed her eyes for a moment, as though visualizing the impact of what was about to happen. "I am sorry to have worried the people in my office who cared about me. Please tell them so. This was just the only way out for me, and maybe it was the wrong way, but I am happy now. I want them to know that."

Elizabeth smiled at her. "We'll tell them."

SIXTEEN

Michael arrived at Dalton's corporate offices shortly before nine, leaving Elizabeth to rest and pack before their departure for Atlanta. They were homesick for Katie and Oak Shadows and had decided to head home.

Mrs. Billings, Wyn's efficient secretary, looked startled by Michael's unannounced visit.

"If you haven't called him, I doubt that he can see you," she said, her business voice firmly in place. "He's in a board meeting and—"

"Oh, I think he'll see me," Michael said, looking her directly in the eye. "Particularly if you tell him I've found Mary Chamblis."

The woman's composure dissolved in a split second. She gasped, staring wide-eyed at Michael for a stunned moment; then she flew out of the room.

Michael wandered into Wyn's office and took his usual seat. As he looked around the impressive office, he thought of what a fraud this man really was, of how he had used and abused Mary, of how he had cheated his own company.

Michael heard footsteps rapidly approaching, but he did not stand. Wyn burst into the room, looking around wildly. "Where's Mary?" he asked.

"She's in North Carolina, but I would advise you not to try to see her. She asked me to tell you that if you leave her alone, she won't file a complaint against you or cause any scandal."

Wyn's mouth flew open. Despite the expensive suit, the

usual impressive tie, the gleam of his imported shoes, Wyn seemed to shrink before Michael's probing stare. Michael realized he had disliked this man almost from the beginning. His instincts had been operating better than he had realized; he just hadn't wanted to admit how he really felt.

Wyn walked over and slammed the door. "What are you talking about? And what makes you think I'll believe you've found her without proof that she's alive?"

"Oh, I have proof," Michael said. "Two other people were with me yesterday when she told us all about your little disagreement at Painted Rock."

Wyn's face darkened. Saying nothing, he walked around the desk and sank into his chair. Then he looked across at Michael. "Would you care to explain that statement?"

"I'll be glad to. Here's the deal. If you agree never to come near her again, she agrees not to press charges against you for physical abuse—"

"Wait a minute!"

"—or for taking the twenty thousand dollars from this company to pay off a gambling debt in Las Vegas."

Wyn slumped deeper in the chair. His mouth sagged as he glared at Michael. "She said that?"

"Yes. And I'd say you'll be pretty lucky to get out of it that easily. If you don't agree to these terms, she'll return to Knoxville with an interesting story for the newspapers."

Wyn's eyes narrowed as a flush crept up his neck to stain his cheeks. "You're enjoying this, aren't you?"

"I never enjoy seeing a man bully a woman, and that's what you've done for a long time. But it's over now. So—" he came to his feet—"you can go back to your board meeting with your reputation intact. However, there has to be a legally binding agreement that you will never try to see her or talk to her again."

"Why should I want to see her? Or talk to her?" Wyn hissed, allowing his ugly temper to surface. "She was a nobody, and she still is, without my help."

"She doesn't need your *help* anymore. She would like for the people in her department who cared about her to know that she's safe but that she's left the state and won't be back."

"That's fine with me," Wyn snapped.

"Then our meeting is concluded," Michael said, his tone now tinged with indifference. He turned and walked to the door, and just as he opened it, he turned his head slightly so that Wyn could hear him clearly. "I'll send you the bill."

He enjoyed his parting shot too much to look back over his shoulder. He shoved his hands into his pockets and strolled out of the corporate offices of Dalton Chemicals, thinking he had never realized how stuffy the place was. At the elevator, he jabbed the button and glanced at the glossy leaves of a huge green fern overflowing a corner table. *Artificial,* he thought. *Like Wyn Dalton.* He stepped onto the elevator and pressed the down button, glad that his job was over.

When Michael arrived back at the chalet, Elizabeth had everything packed and was raring to go.

"Tell me," she said as soon as he entered the living room.

"About what?" Michael asked innocently.

"About Wyn Dalton, of course. Don't you dare tease me either. You know I've been pacing the floor, waiting for you to return with the details!"

Michael laughed as his eyes roamed down her traveling attire. Jeans and a blue turtleneck sweater that accented her beauty and somehow made him think of Katie.

"Am I allowed a cup of coffee before we hit the road?" he

asked, glancing toward the kitchen.

"I already anticipated that you might need some caffeine, so I have the coffeemaker loaded and ready to go." She dashed into the kitchen and flipped the switch on the coffeemaker. Pulling down two mugs from the cabinet, she whirled back to him as the coffee brewed. "Now tell me—what did you say and what did he say and—well, you know the drill."

"I know the drill," he said, rolling his eyes in mock frustration, but he was secretly pleased that Elizabeth had become so caught up in his work.

Carefully he related every detail of his meeting with Wyn Dalton, including the way his formal secretary had almost stumbled over her own feet in her haste to summon Dalton. He elaborated on every moment, enjoying the occasional bursts of laughter that erupted from Elizabeth when she heard how Wyn Dalton had been first stunned, then furious, then humiliated.

"You know, there was something about him that always put me on edge," she said, pouring coffee for them.

"You too?"

She studied Michael over the rim of her mug. "If you had the same feeling, why didn't you share that feeling with me?"

He sipped at the coffee, closing his eyes in pure bliss. "Coffee in the mountains. We're going to miss this. As to why I didn't share my feelings, I really hate being disloyal to my employer."

Elizabeth was shaking her head. "What a wimp he really is! Without his money and power, where would he be?"

Michael shrugged. "It's pretty easy to tell others not to judge, to forgive, all the usual platitudes. Maybe we'd better take that approach ourselves. After all, Raven seemed willing to forgive and forget when we left yesterday."

Elizabeth's brown eyes softened as she looked across the counter at Michael. "Yeah. And I'm glad you agreed to come back to Cherokee and bring Katie next summer. But I have a feeling we may get an invitation before then."

"An invitation?"

"A wedding invitation," she said smugly.

"Ah, that. I'm inclined to agree. When I left Dalton's office, I called Ben to deliver the news. He couldn't wait to get to Raven's place. He said it meant everything to both of them to know that she was free from Wyn Dalton at last."

"Well," Elizabeth said, draining her cup, "it's about check-out time. Which route are we taking back to Atlanta?"

Michael hesitated. "Let's go back through Angel Valley. I really think we should stop in at Matt and Laurel's shop and bring them up to date on what happened."

"I'm glad you think that. So do I."

An hour later Michael and Elizabeth were seated with Matt and Laurel in the private office of their popular shop.

"Tell me," said Laurel, eyes twinkling, "what did Jasper say when you informed him that Mary Chamblis had not been dragged off to a bear's den? That's been his theory, you know."

"And a cruel one, at that," Elizabeth added.

"He and Sheriff Grayson were both just relieved to learn that she was alive. They're going to pass the word along to the merchants here and in Cherokee that Mary has been located. But they promised to respect her privacy."

"Do you think Wyn Dalton will keep his word about not trying to see her?" Matt asked.

"I think he had better. Otherwise he'll have Ben and the Cherokee citizens to answer to, not to mention a court of law in Knoxville. I feel sure Wyn Dalton is out of Mary's life for good."

Laurel smiled, looking immensely pleased. "This calls for a celebration. Are you sure you two can't stay for lunch?"

"Really, we can't," Michael answered. "We need to get on the road."

"We're really missing Katie," Elizabeth added.

"Yeah, I'm sure you are." Matt smiled at them.

"Matt, you'll let us know when Laurel goes into the hospital, won't you? Michael and I have a wager on whether you're having a boy or a girl," Elizabeth reported.

"Oh?" Laurel tilted her head, sending her blond brown hair in a swirl about her face. "Care to share your opinion on which one we're getting?"

Michael and Elizabeth exchanged an amused glance; then Elizabeth smiled at Laurel. "If you have a boy, he buys my dinner; if you have a girl, I buy his."

Matt and Laurel looked at each other and laughed. Then Matt reached for Laurel's hand and gently lifted her fingers to his lips. "We just want a healthy baby. And then I'll buy everyone's dinner."

Everyone laughed at that as Michael and Elizabeth stood to say good-bye. Michael shook hands with Matt and Elizabeth hugged Laurel. "You know, I feel as though I have known you all my life," Elizabeth said, smiling down at Laurel, who was shorter by a few inches. "Jessica told me everyone loves you. I can see why."

"Well, Mary Chamblis is not the only one indebted to you two," Laurel said, hugging Elizabeth again. "We're all relieved to know that she's safe and that no criminals are lurking around our area, ready to grab someone for ransom money. I can tell you, it's given Matt and me some cause for worry."

"But no more," Matt said, putting an arm around Laurel. "You two drive carefully."

"Thanks. We will."

As they walked back through the huge display of arts and crafts, Michael slanted a quizzical look at Elizabeth. "You mean you don't want to do some last minute shopping?"

"Nope." She shook her head and placed her hand in the crook of Michael's arm.

"I'm perfectly satisfied. Not only do I have the most wonderful husband in the world, and the most charming daughter..." She paused as Michael opened the door for her. "I've now earned a new career for myself if the occasion arrives."

Michael arched an eyebrow. "A new career? What is it?"

"Why, as a private detective, of course. Admit it; I cracked the case."

Michael threw his head back and laughed as they walked to the Blazer. "Must you always be right?" he teased, opening her door.

"No. Just this once."

He was still laughing when he got behind the wheel and they drove out of the peaceful little paradise known as Angel Valley.

Dear Reader,

As I wrote this book, I kept longing to be deep in the mountains, surrounded by lush valleys and foggy mists like the characters in *Spirits* were. Even more, I longed to meet the people who have only been characters in the Calloway stories for the past two years. While most of these people are fictional, I have come to think of them as "family," and I hope that you have, as well. More important, I hope that the stories in the Calloway novels have given you some insight or inspiration for your daily struggles and joys, and that somehow these people and their settings have brought you closer to God.

As always, my deep love for Tennessee, my home state, and the beautiful Smoky Mountains almost took over the story. I am indebted to the people of Sevierville, Pigeon Forge, and Gatlinburg for opening their homes and hearts to me.

Thanks for making the journey with me.

To God be the glory.

Peggy Darty

PALISADES...PURE ROMANCE

⁓ PALISADES ⁓

Reunion, Karen Ball
Refuge, Lisa Tawn Bergren
Torchlight, Lisa Tawn Bergren
Treasure, Lisa Tawn Bergren
Chosen, Lisa Tawn Bergren
Firestorm, Lisa Tawn Bergren
Surrender, Lynn Bulock
Dalton's Dilemma, Lynn Bulock
Wise Man's House, Melody Carlson
Heartland Skies, Melody Carlson
Shades of Light, Melody Carlson
Cherish, Constance Colson
Chase the Dream, Constance Colson
Angel Valley, Peggy Darty
Sundance, Peggy Darty
Moonglow, Peggy Darty
Promises, Peggy Darty
Memories, Peggy Darty
Spirits, Peggy Darty
Remembering the Roses, Marion Duckworth
Love Song, Sharon Gillenwater
Antiques, Sharon Gillenwater
Texas Tender, Sharon Gillenwater
Secrets, Robin Jones Gunn
Whispers, Robin Jones Gunn
Echoes, Robin Jones Gunn
Sunsets, Robin Jones Gunn
Clouds, Robin Jones Gunn

Waterfalls, Robin Jones Gunn
Coming Home, Barbara Jean Hicks
Snow Swan, Barbara Jean Hicks
China Doll, Barbara Jean Hicks
Angel in the Senate, Kristen Johnson Ingram
Irish Eyes, Annie Jones
Father by Faith, Annie Jones
Irish Rogue, Annie Jones
Beloved, Deb Kastner
Glory, Marilyn Kok
On Assignment, Marilyn Kok
Sierra, Shari MacDonald
Forget-Me-Not, Shari MacDonald
Diamonds, Shari MacDonald
Stardust, Shari MacDonald
Westward, Amanda MacLean
Stonehaven, Amanda MacLean
Everlasting, Amanda MacLean
Kingdom Come, Amanda MacLean
Betrayed, Lorena McCourtney
Escape, Lorena McCourtney
Dear Silver, Lorena McCourtney
Forgotten, Lorena McCourtney
Canyon, Lorena McCourtney
Rustlers, Karen Rispin
Enough! Gayle Roper
The Key, Gayle Roper
The Document, Gayle Roper
Voyage, Elaine Schulte

Anthologies
A Christmas Joy, Darty, Gillenwater, MacLean
Mistletoe, Ball, Hicks, McCourtney
A Mother's Love, Bergren, Colson, MacLean
Silver Bells, Bergren, Krause, MacDonald
Heart's Delight, Ball, Hicks, Noble
Fools for Love, Ball, Brooks, Jones